THE ECONOMICS OF WAGE CONTROLS

Also by K. Holden, D. A. Peel and J. L. Thompson

MODELLING THE UK ECONOMY
EXPECTATIONS: Theory and Evidence

The Economics of Wage Controls

K. Holden
Senior Lecturer in Economics
University of Liverpool

D. A. Peel
Professor of Economics
University College, Aberystwyth

and

J. L. Thompson
Senior Lecturer in Economics
Liverpool Polytechnic

St. Martin's Press   New York

First published in the United States of America in 1987

Printed in Hong Kong

ISBN 0-312-23654-9

Library of Congress Cataloging-in-Publication Data

Holden, K.
The economics of wage controls.
Bibliography: p.
1. Wage–price policy. 2. Wage–price policy—Case
studies. I. Peel, D. A. II. Thompson, John L.
III. Title.
HC79. W24H65 1986   331.2′1   86–11813
ISBN 0-312-23654-9

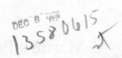

To Jennifer, Janet and Margaret

Contents

Preface

This book is intended as an introduction to the economics of wage and price controls (or incomes policies) for undergraduates taking courses in macroeconomics and the labour market. The first chapter reviews the historical experience of controls in a number of countries. In Chapter 2 the ways in which economists assess the impact of conventional incomes policies are considered along with the empirical evidence relating to their success. Recently different forms of tax-based incomes policy and arbitration methods have been suggested. These are analysed in Chapters 3 and 4. The economics of indexation are presented in Chapter 5 and some policy conclusions discussed in the final chapter.

A list of references is included at the end of the text. We acknowledge financial assistance from the Economic and Social Research Council (Grant B00232056) in the preliminary stages of preparing the manuscript. Our thanks are also due to Vivienne Oakes for her accurate and efficient typing of several drafts of the text. As always, any errors and omissions are the responsibility of the authors.

K. Holden
D. A. Peel
J. L. Thompson

1 Recent Experience with Wage and Price Controls

1.1 INTRODUCTION

Since the end of the Second World War, various western governments have attempted, by legal restraints or moral persuasion, to influence the way in which aggregate wages and/or prices change. Such actions are known as incomes policies or wage and price controls. In this chapter we review the recent experience of a number of countries in order to provide the background for the assessment of conventional incomes policies in Chapter 2. First, in section 1.2 we examine the attempts to impose wage and price controls in Germany in the thirties, under the Nazi government. Next we consider the postwar experience of incomes policies in the United Kingdom, the United States, New Zealand and Australia and conclude with references to studies of other countries.

Wage and price controls have generally been invoked at times when governments believe that either the rate of inflation is too high or it is increasing too rapidly. The intention is to reduce inflation directly by operating on wages and prices: if prices are fixed there is no inflation. Indirect methods of controlling inflation, such as by deflating aggregate demand or reducing monetary growth, are thought to be more costly, in terms of lost output and higher unemployment, by advocates of controls (see, for example, Layard, 1982; Meade, 1985).

1.2 HISTORICAL REVIEW

The idea that governments can control the absolute or relative level of wages and prices has a long history. Schuettinger (1982) refers to the Egyptian government controlling the grain crop 5000 years ago and the Code of Hammurabi imposing rigid controls over wages and prices in Babylon around 2000 BC. Schuettinger reviews controls in Ancient Greece, the Roman Empire, Medieval Europe, the early days of Canada and the United States, Russia after the revolution, Germany in the thirties and during the First and Second World Wars. Here we will not duplicate all that material but instead consider what happened under the

1

Nazi regime in Germany. This time is of particular interest because the state had enormous powers at its disposal to make a prices and incomes policy effective in contrast to the countries considered below which are democracies, the activities of whose governments are constrained by their legal systems.

Economic policy in the Third Reich is discussed by Brittan and Lilley (1977), Schweitzer (1964), Lurie (1947), Schoenbaum (1967) and Schuettinger (1982). After the Wall Street crash of 1929 American loans and investment in Germany stopped and at the same time the demand for German goods overseas collapsed. The German economy entered a severe depression. In 1931 emergency decrees were issued which would allow the government to control prices. The banks were taken over by the government and currency controls were imposed to stop the mark collapsing. Unemployment rose from 1.3 million in September 1929 to 2.3 million in March 1930 and to over 6 million in March 1932. In the elections of July 1932 the National Socialists won 230 out of the 608 seats and, following much political manoeuvring, Hitler was appointed Reich Chancellor in January 1933. A four-year plan was announced involving government works using initially voluntary and, after 1935, conscripted labour. This was financed partly by higher taxes, partly by increased government debt and also by printing money. The money supply increased by 70 per cent between 1933 and 1938. The increase in economic activity put pressure on prices and wages. In earlier periods prices had been set by cartels. The government strengthened these by giving them legal powers to fix and enforce prices and the 'Law of Compulsory Cartels' of 1933 allowed the authorities to extend any cartel to include extra enterprises. The government also took a more direct role in supervising the cartels. The result was that many prices were directly controlled and the monopoly position of the cartels was strengthened.

However, the balance of trade had been deteriorating since 1931 because of the general reduction in world trade. By 1934 reserves of gold and foreign exchange were almost exhausted and strict import controls were imposed. In February 1934 German importers were allowed to spend 50 per cent of the amount of foreign exchange they had spent in 1931. By May 1934 this was reduced to 5 per cent. The shortage of imported goods raised their prices. At the same time new methods of cost calculation were approved which allowed some cost increases to be passed on. While world prices rose by 1.6 per cent between 1933 and 1936, the official price index in Germany rose by 7 per cent, despite the attempts to hold down prices. Low relative prices of agricultural products led to reduced farm output because of the movement of labour to towns, so that, for example, butter was in short supply in 1935.

When the Nazis took power they dissolved the trade unions and in 1934 the Labour Regulation act was passed which banned strikes and lockouts. The government set up Labour Trustees to set minimum wages, subject to the official policy of keeping most wages at their 1933 level. Legally employers could pay more than this but did not do so. The result was a decline in real wages between 1933 and 1937. In 1934 laws were passed placing restrictions on the movement of labour. Workers in agriculture were not allowed to move into urban areas. While initially such restrictions were to prevent unemployment they became part of a more general policy of state control. From 1936 all workers had to have a 'work book' which acted as an identification document and gave the state details of the individual workers' qualifications and experience. With the expansion of the economy, as a result of government works and rearmament, intervention increased. Workers could not be hired without approval of the regional labour offices. Even with these controls skilled workers were in short supply in several industries by 1936.

Pressure for wage and price increases was building up so in November 1936 a general wage and price freeze was imposed. Some flexibility was permitted in pricing and many government contracts were based on cost agreements. Shortages continued and wage ceilings were used by Labour Trustees to prevent competitive bidding for skilled labour. Between 1933 and 1939 wage rates were almost unchanged in money terms, increasing from 78.5 *Pf.* per hour to 79 *Pf.* per hour. Earnings rose because of increases in the number of hours worked and a shift towards piece-rate payments.

A second four-year plan was announced in the autumn of 1936 with the intention of making Germany entirely self-sufficient in food and industrial raw materials. This reduced unemployment so that by 1938 full employment prevailed. New labour reserves were opened up by the conquest of Austria, Sudetenland and parts of Czechoslovakia. These were incorporated into the German work force. Labour shortages became a serious problem and threatened Hitler's military plans. The final steps to prevent the free movement of labour were taken in 1938 when a decree was passed ordering all workers to take a new job if required. As a further step towards removing labour shortages, those leaving school were directed into apprenticeships useful to the state. Even with all these powers to direct labour, skilled workers continued to be in short supply at the fixed wage rates.

The conclusion from the experience of Germany in the thirties is that wage and price controls resulted in shortages of labour and goods. Moreover, despite all the attempts by the state to control economic activity, the work-force reacted to fixed wages by moving to areas of the economy where rewards were highest (i.e. from farms to factories and from fixed wages to piece-rate payments).

1.3 THE UNITED KINGDOM

Since the end of the Second World War there have been a number of incomes policies in the United Kingdom; in fact between July 1961 and May 1979 the only time there was no form of incomes policy in operation was from July 1970 to July 1971. Details of the various policies are provided by Ingham (1981) and Fishbein (1984) with Flanagan, Soskice and Ulman (1983) and Dean (1981) providing summaries for parts of the period. The exchange rate was fixed from 1949 to 1967 and there was a belief in some quarters that an incomes policy would allow the simultaneous achievement of stable prices and a higher rate of growth (and lower unemployment) than could be achieved by fiscal or monetary policy alone.

Two features of the UK economy are important: the industrial relations system and the role of the public sector. In the postwar period the system of wage determination has been for basic rates of pay to be negotiated for each industry between employers' federations and national unions. This is then followed by local negotiations between small groups of workers, represented by the shop steward, and their supervisors. Since the late sixties there has been a move towards plant-wide and company-wide bargaining, but the national negotiations still have an important function in setting the mood for the local negotiations.

In 1970 the public sector accounted for 25 per cent of total employment according to *Economic Trends* November 1979. This was made up of 6.3 per cent central government, 10.5 per cent local government (including police, teachers, fire service, municipal transport) and 8.3 per cent public corporations (including gas, electricity, water, post office, railway and coal mining workers). The size of this sector and the fact that the government either controls or can strongly influence its level of wages means that even with free collective bargaining the government plays an important role in wage determination.

The 1948 Wage Freeze and 1956 Plateau

Following the end of the Second World War the Labour Party won its first general election in 1945. There were still widespread price controls and rationing and many products were unavailable or in short supply. When the economy switched to peacetime production the balance of payments position deteriorated and inflation accelerated, leading to an appeal by the government in January 1947 for higher productivity and, later that year, for voluntary wage restraint. As this did not occur, a wage freeze was announced in February 1948 in which the only exceptions were to be in industries with a shortage of labour. Prices would remain frozen and the wage freeze was to be compulsory in the public sector and voluntary elsewhere. Following discussions, dividends were also controlled, and the Trades Union Congress (TUC) supported the freeze at a special conference in 1948, and its annual conferences in 1948 and 1949. In 1950, however, the TUC rejected wage restraint because of rank and file discontent with the policy. There were three main reasons for this, according to Fishbein (1984); real wages had fallen between 1948 and 1950, the devaluation of sterling in 1949 was expected to raise prices, and the freeze had operated unevenly in that hourly paid workers received no increases while piece-work workers were able to raise their incomes by increasing output. It is generally agreed that the freeze reduced the rate of increase of wages and that much of its success came from the desire of union leaders to help the Labour government in the particular circumstances of the immediate post-war period.

The boom associated with the Korean War of 1950 and the relaxation of wartime price controls and subsidies by the new Conservative government elected in 1951, coupled with free collective bargaining, led to an increase in inflation in the early fifties. This was controlled by fiscal policy but the economic revival in 1955 further boosted inflation. The government introduced the Macmillan 'price and wage plateau' in March 1956. The nationalised industries and a number of private employers agreed not to increase prices. There was no arrangement to restrain wages directly but the assumption was that there would be less pressure for wage increases if prices were steady. The policy lasted until January 1957 when free collective bargaining was resumed.

The Pay Pause 1961–2 and Guiding Light 1962–5

The Conservative government continued free collective bargaining in the late fifties with a policy of deflating the economy as a means of keeping prices under control. An independent body, the Council on Prices, Productivity and Income (CPPI) was set up in 1957 to provide comment on economic policy, particularly concerning prices and wages. It proposed that, in general, there should be a link between changes in pay and changes in productivity. In its final report in 1961 the CPPI recommended some form of incomes policy to reduce inflation. There was a balance of payments crisis at this time and the Chancellor, Selwyn Lloyd, introduced a 'pay pause' which would freeze wages in the public sector and rely on voluntary support in the private sector. Existing commitments to increases could be honoured and the government was to try to develop a more permanent way of relating productivity increases and wage increases. The TUC opposed the pay pause and, because groups such as teachers and nurses suffered under it, while less popular but better organised groups benefited from it, the policy was largely ineffective and ended early in 1962. A new body, the National Incomes Commission (NIC) was set up with the job of investigating particular cases of proposed wage increases referred to it by the government. The NIC was intended to be independent of the government, employers and unions and was expected to encourage employer resistance to wage increases. A 'guiding light' allowing increases of between 2 and 2.5 per cent in wages was suggested for 1962, with further increases permissible where productivity increases were involved or where the industry was short of labour. The TUC did not co-operate with the NIC since there was no attempt to control prices. Early in 1963 the target rate of wage change was raised from 3 to 3.5 per cent. Along with the NIC, in 1962 the government set up the National Economic Development Council ('NEDDY'), chaired by the Chancellor of the Exchequer and with government, employer and union representatives. Since the unions were not participating in the NIC, the role of NEDDY became important as a point of contact with the government. Initially NEDDY was concerned with stimulating economic growth but in 1963 it published a report, agreed by the union representatives, acknowledging that wages, salaries and profits would need to rise less rapidly than in the past. The government presented an expansionary budget to encourage economic growth, which persuaded the TUC representatives on NEDDY to discuss the possibility of a voluntary incomes policy. In the end no agreement was reached but the crucial link between restraining wage demands and economic expansion was now established. The 'guiding light' policy ended with the election of a Labour government in October 1964.

Restraint under Labour 1964–70

Following the election, inflation was increasing because of the 1963 expansionary budget and there was a high balance of payments deficit. The NIC was abolished and a *Joint Statement of Intent on Productivity Prices and Incomes* was agreed by the TUC and the government, while a voluntary incomes policy with a 3 to 3.5 per cent norm continued. The government created the Department of Economic Affairs which was to be responsible for increasing the long-term rate of growth. A National Board for Prices and Incomes (NBPI) was set up in February 1965 with the job of advising the government whether proposed increases in prices and wages were in the national interest. In April 1965 the government announced its Prices and Incomes Policy, a voluntary policy with a wage norm of 3 to 3.5 per cent and exceptional increases allowed for increased productivity, labour shortages, low pay and comparability. The TUC accepted the policy but wage and price inflation continued. Wages rose by 8.3 and 8.5 per cent in 1964 and 1965, while the corresponding figures for prices were 3.2 and 4.8 per cent. There was a balance of payments crisis in July 1965 which resulted in the government announcing legislation to make prior notification of wage and price increases to the NBPI compulsory.

The TUC acted to avoid government wage controls by setting up its own system for vetting proposed wage increases. However, a further balance of payments crisis in July 1966 resulted in the statutory *Prices and Incomes Standstill* which included a mandatory six-month freeze on all wages, prices and dividends, to be followed by a six-month period of severe restraint. At the same time the government imposed strongly deflationary fiscal and monetary policies. During the freeze period only productivity increases could justify any wage increase, and a particular feature was that any commitments to increases which had not been implemented when the policy was announced were also frozen. For the period of severe restraint (January – July 1967) the norm was again zero but productivity increases, low pay, labour shortages and comparability could all justify an increase in wages. Prices could only rise to cover tax and cost increases beyond the control of the firm. Between July 1966 and July 1967, unemployment rose from 1.3 to 1.8 per cent, hourly wage rates rose 2.8 per cent and consumer prices rose by 2.5 per cent. These increases were much lower than during the preceding year so to some extent the policy worked. No major union attempted to evade the freeze, possibly because of the wish to avoid a confrontation with a determined Labour government.

From July 1967 to March 1968 a policy of moderate restraint was planned, during which productivity deals were promoted, a minimum period of twelve months was imposed between settlements and, if these criteria were satisfied, increases might be made in stages. Proposals for price and wage increases continued to be referred to the NBPI if they appeared to violate the criteria. Sterling was devalued by 14 per cent in November 1967 and the government tightened fiscal and monetary policy.

As one of the effects of devaluation is to increase the price of imports, inflation was expected to rise so wage restraint became even more necessary than previously. However, the TUC took a different view, arguing for a rapid expansion to boost investment and exports, coupled with its voluntary incomes policy. As there was only a small majority within the TUC for the voluntary policy the government announced in March 1968 a statutory limit for wages and dividends of 3.5 per cent per annum for the period to December 1969. This ceiling was to apply to groups of workers covered by a single settlement so that some flexibility was available. In practice the 3.5 per cent figure became a minimum, with productivity increases (of differing validity) justifying larger amounts. Earnings rose by 8.1 per cent in 1968 and by 8.3 per cent in 1969. The final phase of this government's incomes policy came with the announcement in December 1969 of a range of 2.5 to 4.5 per cent for pay increases and the abandonment of dividend restraint. The main features of the earlier pay policies continued – productivity and low pay allowing higher wage increases – with pay relativities and equal pay for women being additional factors. There was a wages and prices 'explosion' which continued after the Conservative victory in the June 1970 general election. While this might indicate the policies had failed, it could equally be argued that the 'explosion' occurred because of their initial success.

The Heath Government Policies 1971–4

The new Conservative government, headed by Edward Heath, was committed to not introducing an incomes policy. However, by mid-1970 the rate of increase of earnings was 13 per cent and unemployment reached 3.6 per cent, which was high by postwar standards. The government approach was to put pressure on public sector negotiators to reduce pay awards. The strategy, known as the 'n−1' policy, relied on the increase in wages for each group being 1 per cent below the previous settlement, and became effective in mid-1971. At the same time deflationary policies were adopted and unemployment rose to 3.5 per cent in 1971 and 3.9 per cent in 1972. There was also a voluntary commitment by the employers to restrain price increases to 5 per cent. The NBPI was abolished in March 1971. The 'n–1' policy had some success with postal and National Health Service workers in 1971 but the coal miners received a 20 per cent increase after a strike in 1972 which caused a national state of emergency to be declared and prolonged electricity cuts to be imposed. When the railway workers received a 13 per cent increase compared to their previous settlement of 9 per cent, the 'n–1' policy was dropped.

The Prime Minister attempted to reach a voluntary agreement with unions on pay and prices between the spring and autumn of 1972 without success. In June 1972 the pound was floated and since the money supply was growing at over 20 per cent per annum there was a danger of a rapid depreciation of its value. The government decided that an incomes policy was required and in November 1972 a ninety-day freeze of wages, prices, dividends and rents was announced and became known as Stage I of the policy. In April 1973 Stage II started with a target of £1 per week plus 4 per cent, subject to a maximum of £250 for any individual. As with the last Labour policy, the norm applied to groups rather than to each worker. Extra increases were permitted in the reduction of male/female pay differentials. A minimum period of twelve months was required between wage increases. Stage II lasted until November 1973 and was followed by Stage III which had a norm of the larger of 7 per cent or £2.25, and extra increases allowed for productivity agreements, working unsocial hours and to remove anomalies. There was also scope for 'threshold payments' or 'escalator' clauses whereby if the retail price index increased by more than 7 per cent over its October 1973 figure workers would receive 40p per week for each 1 per cent rise. A Pay Board and a Price Commission were set up at the end of 1973 with authority to control wages and prices. (Compare equivalent developments in the USA under the New Economic Policy 1971–4 in section 1.4 below.) The TUC refused to nominate trade union representatives to these bodies. The Pay Board had to be advised of any settlements effecting more than 100 workers and advance approval was required if more than 1000 workers were to be affected. Firms with fewer than 100 workers were required to keep pay records. If a settlement did not meet the requirements of the pay policy the Pay Board could reject it. Inflation continued in 1973 because of three factors: the drop in the value of the pound, the rise in oil and commodity prices and the effects of the 'Barber boom' (expansionary budgets in 1971 and 1972). Whereas the government had expected inflation of about 7 per cent in 1974, the outcome was 17 per cent so that threshold payments of £4.40 per week were being paid by October 1974. During Stage III many groups reached settlements at or around the government-approved levels. The coal miners however, called for a 30 per cent increase at a time when, because of the October 1973 Middle East War, oil prices had risen and coal was in high demand. When the government refused to grant this increase an overtime ban was imposed and from January 1974 the government reduced electricity supplies to commercial users to three days per week. The miners announced a national strike to begin in February and the government then resigned and called on the people to support their tough approach to the miners. The Conservatives were defeated and Labour took over as a minority government.

The Social Contract 1974–9

The new Labour government continued the Stage III policies in their first months in office with the addition of a new category of 'special cases' who were allowed high increases. The miners and nurses benefited from this. The initial budget, in March 1974 was mildly deflationary and in response to rising unemployment and in preparation for an autumn election a mini-budget in July 1974 cut indirect taxes. The Labour Party won the election with a small majority and another budget was introduced which was mildly reflationary. Since 1973 the Labour Party and the TUC had been discussing policies for controlling inflation and achieving economic growth. They were committed to a voluntary agreement in which unions would restrain wage demands in exchange for various social measures. This was known as the Social Contract and relied on 'responsible' collective bargaining and statutory price controls. The Pay Board was abolished in July 1974, and a number of large increases were made to public sector groups in the year after the election. The rate of earnings increase exceeded 30 per cent by the end of 1974 and inflation passed 25 per cent in May 1975. By spring 1975 the government and TUC had realised the original Social Contract had failed and a sterling crisis in June prompted them to reach agreement on Phase I of a formal pay policy in July 1975. This allowed a maximum increase of £6 per week per worker with nothing for those earning more than £8500.

The policy was voluntary but the government threatened to make it statutory if this became necessary. There were no serious challenges to this policy by the unions and the annual percentage wage increase dropped from 27.6 in July 1975 to 13.9 in July 1976. In the budget of April 1976 the government proposed personal income tax cuts which would only be implemented if the TUC accepted a Phase II incomes policy with a norm of 3 per cent. The actual agreement, for the year from 1 August 1976 was for increases of between £2.50 and £4 with a maximum of 5 per cent. Price controls would also be relaxed. For the last six months of 1976 wages rose at an annual rate of 10.6 per cent while for the first half of 1977 this dropped to 6.0 per cent. Phase III of the Social Contract was from August 1977 to July 1978 and allowed a maximum increase in earnings of 10 per cent. This came after various unions had voted for free collective bargaining and the TUC had said it could only support the continuation of the rule of twelve months occurring between settlements. The Phase III policy was enforced by refusing price increases to firms exceeding the target. Most unions complied with the Phase III policy. In July 1978 the government unilaterally imposed Phase IV, with a maximum increase of 5 per cent. The TUC and the employers had refused to co-operate in further policies and as a result the government had severe problems in carrying it through. There were a large number of strikes in support of higher wages in the 'winter of discontent' in January to March 1979. Many public sector groups settled for 9 per cent plus a referral to a comparability commission. In February 1979 a 'concordat' between the government and the unions recognised Phase IV had failed and set a target of 5 per cent inflation by 1982. However by April 1979 the small Labour majority had disappeared in by-elections and following a defeat in the House of Commons an election was called.

Mrs Thatcher won the election and removed all attempts at prices and incomes policies, relying on 'cash limits' to keep public sector pay under control.

It is difficult to come to any clear conclusions from the experience of wage and price controls in the United Kingdom over the postwar period. Many forms of incomes policies were tried and in general, were terminated by the government when they appeared to be failing. However, this does not mean that the controls had no effect since other things would have happened in their absence. We will return to the problem of evaluating controls in Chapter 2.

1.4   UNITED STATES OF AMERICA

An important feature of the American economy is that there is no national pay bargaining structure and any intervention must be at the microeconomic level. In the postwar period there have been four attempts at incomes policy in the United States. These were during the Korean War, the guideposts of 1962–7, the New Economic Policy of 1971–4 and the Carter administration's Pay and Price Standards 1978–82. The history of these policies is presented in Pencavel (1981), Congressional Budget Office (1977), Mills (1975) and Goodwin (1975).

The Korean War Controls

The Korean War started in June 1950 and the government initially aimed to meet the increased military spending without wage and price controls and at the same time keep taxes and interest rates low. However, some consumers and businesses, which had been subjected to controls during the Second World War and in the postwar period until July 1949, attempted to buy goods and increase inventories in anticipation of future controls. There was an immediate increase in consumer demand, an increase in profits and a willingness of employers to grant large wage increases. The inflation rate rose and in July 1950 President Truman asked for emergency legislation, passed in September 1950, which would give the administration the power to control wages and prices, and at the same time to take various measures to boost military production. Two agencies were set up: the Office of Price Stability (OPS), a government body to control prices, and the Wage Stabilization Board (WSB), representing industry, labour and the public, to control wages. One part of the legislation concerned voluntary restraint on prices and wages but there was also scope for price ceilings to be enforced and wages to be stabilized. Credit was also to be limited. In December 1950 details of the new controls were announced. Voluntary pricing standards were introduced and several hundred large firms were asked to give notice of price increases. Originally the only mandatory controls were on new car prices and the wages of auto-workers but early in 1951 an excess profits tax was imposed on increases of corporate profits over a prewar base period. This was thought to be anti-inflationary since it reduced the funds available for expansion and also meant that firms were less able to pay for large wage increases. By the end of January 1951 a general wage and price freeze was imposed because of the increasing inflation rate and the problems with voluntary controls. Steps were also taken to guide output to areas useful for defence purposes and to prevent hoarding. It was recognised that the wage freeze was having an uneven effect on the labour market: some agreements giving large wage increases just avoided the freeze while in other cases the freeze prevented negotiations reaching an agreement. Within a few weeks the freeze of both prices and wages was relaxed to allow wage increases of up to 10 per cent more than the January 1950 figure with other increases being allowed as special cases. Some cost pass-through into prices was permitted from April 1951 and in July further relaxations of the freeze on prices were agreed.

The view of the labour members of the WSB in February 1951 was that wages were being held down more than prices and so they withdrew from the scheme. The WSB continued in various forms until early in 1953. The immediate cause of the collapse of controls was a September 1952 recommendation by the WSB that coal miners should receive an increase of $1.50 per day when the United Mine Workers and coal employers had agreed on $1.90 per day. The miners went on strike in October and, almost two months later, President Truman intervened to approve the higher increase. The chairman and industry members of the WSB resigned and the formal end of controls came after the presidential election.

The evidence on the effectiveness of the Korean War controls is mixed. Before the freeze on wages and prices in January 1951 the inflation rate had increased sharply but this was at least partly in anticipation of future controls. Once the controls were in force both wage and price inflation declined: in the case of the consumer price index the annual rate of increase of almost 17 per cent in early 1951 was below 5 per cent by the end of the year. It would be premature to attribute this decline to the effects of the controls. It is necessary first to have some measure of what would have happened to wages and prices in the absence of controls. This is a subtle exercise which we consider more fully in Chapter 2.

The Guideposts 1962–8

The US economy grew slowly during the late 1950s and early 1960s, unemployment was high and the balance of payments was deteriorating. In 1962 the Kennedy administration tried to stimulate the economy by expansionary monetary and fiscal policies. Simultaneously, because of fears of inflation the President's Council of Economic Advisers (CEA) announced a wage–price guideposts policy whereby voluntary standards for wage and price increases would apply. In the case of wages, the rate of increase of wage rates, including fringe benefits, in each industry was to equal the trend rate of productivity increase in the economy as a whole. Exceptions were to be allowed if there were labour shortages or low wages compared to similar jobs elsewhere. For prices, depending on whether the industry's rate of productivity increase was above, equal to, or below the overall rate, prices should fall, be unchanged or rise in proportion. The only permitted exceptions were for industries in which profits were not sufficient to attract the required capital. The policy was voluntary and since the CEA was responsible for formulating the policy no new agency was needed for this purpose.

Mills (1975) points out three characteristics of the guideposts policy. First, the use of a single figure, the trend rate of productivity increase for the economy as a whole, for wage increases. The flexibility mentioned above was seldom invoked after the first few months of the policy and in fact the productivity increase of 3.2 per cent per year, adopted in 1964, continued to the end of the policy even though a higher figure could have been justified. Secondly, only the executive branch of the federal government was involved in developing and administering the guidelines, in contrast to the Korean War Controls described previously which involved employers, labour and the public, as well as the government. Thirdly, the guideposts were aimed at large firms and unions because of the belief that there is an important part of the economy where wages and prices are not determined competitively but are likely to be sensitive to public opinion so that pressure from the CEA could reduce inflation.

The CEA, with a professional staff of about 20, and many other responsibilities, monitored wage and price changes. Their main sources of information about impending increases were newspapers and television. Many other increases occurred which the CEA never heard about. When an increase above the guideposts was discovered, the CEA attempted to persuade the parties to change their decision. No penalties were available for non-compliance, except occasionally when for example, the Department of Defense was instructed not to place orders with offending firms.

The guideposts were re-stated each year from 1962 to 1966 and in general were complied with. The economy expanded from 1961–4 with real GNP growing at 4.4 per cent per annum and unemployment falling. In 1965, however, expenditure associated with the Vietnam War rose and President Johnson did not increase taxes to restrain aggregate demand. The tightening labour markets increased the number of wage settlements above the guideposts and various strikes occurred. The 3.2 per cent guidepost was adopted again in January 1966 and a major confrontation developed in the summer of that year. The International Association of Machinists organised a strike against five airlines. President Johnson intervened and announced an agreement of a 4.3 per cent increase which he described as non-inflationary since this was the industry's rate of productivity improvement. The union members failed to accept the settlement, resumed the strike and finally accepted 4.9 per cent. This spelt the end of the guideposts since the CEA position was undermined.

In studies of the impact of the guideposts, Perry (1967) and Reid (1981) found evidence supporting the view that the guideposts were effective in reducing inflation over the period 1962–6. Black and Kelejian (1970) and Gordon (1970), however, disagreed with this conclusion. The problem, as always, is to determine what would have happened in the absence of guideposts. While the guideposts appeared to have had some success in 1962–6, many criticisms have been made about the lack of involvement of employers and labour, the use of a single target figure, the lack of adequate administrative support, and the need for machinery to deal with disputes. Also, no one claims any success for the guideposts after 1966.

New Economic Policy 1971–4

After the ending of the wage–price guideposts the American economy continued to expand, partly as a result of the Vietnam War build-up and partly because of the large federal budget deficit of the Johnson administration. When President Nixon took office in 1969 the economy was overheated, with the growth of real output falling and the rate of inflation rising. Monetary and fiscal policies were adopted to reduce the inflation rate but their effect was mainly on output and employment. Public opinion was strongly in favour of price controls to beat inflation and in 1970 the Congress, against President Nixon's wishes, passed an act giving him authority to control prices. He used the powers in March 1971 to set up a board to reduce wage inflation in the construction industry, following a median increase of 17 per cent, but he refused to adopt general controls until there was a balance of payments crisis in August 1971. This resulted in the New Economic Policy (NEP) being introduced which included a temporary 10 per cent surcharge on imports, the ending of the convertibility of gold, a ninety-day freeze on wages, profits and prices (with some agricultural products and goods involved in international trade exempt), and some tax reductions. The idea behind the ninety-day freeze, which became known as Phase I, was to remove inflationary expectations and to allow time to plan the future policy. A cabinet-level committee, the Cost of Living Council (CLC) was formed to administer the controls programme.

The objective of Phase II, starting in November 1971, was to reduce price inflation to 2 to 3 per cent per annum by the end of 1972. A Pay Board, with general public, employer and labour representatives was set up to administer wage controls, and a Price Commission, consisting of members of the public, was to oversee prices and rents. The target for wage increase was 5.5 per cent, based on a 3 per cent productivity increase and a 2.5 per cent cost of living adjustment, and an extra 0.7 per cent was allowed for fringe benefits. There was some flexibility with extra increases permitted for low paid workers, those who had received small increases previously, and to keep essential employees. The Price Commission controlled price increases by allowing input cost rises, adjusted for productivity and volume of output changes, to be passed on in prices, only if profit margins were unchanged. Firms which did not increase prices were able to increase profits and were not affected by the price controls. As with the Korean War different sized firms had to meet different requirements. Three groups referred to as tiers or categories, were identified, with different definitions for the Price Commission or Pay Board. For prices, size was determined by value of sales: Tier I – sales of $100 m and over (1500 firms with 45 per cent of sales); Tier II – sales of $50 m to $100 m (1000 firms with 5 per cent of sales); Tier III – sales of under $50 m (10 m firms with 50 per cent of sales). For wages, size was determined by number of employees; Tier I – 5000 or more (10 per cent of all employees); Tier II – 1000–5000 (7 per cent of all employees); Tier III – less than 1000 (83 per cent of all employees). Firms in Tier I were required to give advance notification of intended changes in prices and pay, while those in Tier II simply reported any changes. Both of these tiers also provided quarterly price, costs and profits reports to the Price Commission. Tier III firms were expected to keep the wage and price regulations and were subject to monitoring and spot checks. Labour participation in the Pay Board continued until March 1972 when they stated that Phase II was a means of holding down wages while allowing prices and profits to increase. The Pay Board was reformed with seven members, the five 'public' members of the original board and two new members with special interests from labour and business.

Phase II continued until January 1973 when Phase III was introduced.

This was intended to be a transitional period between controls and voluntary restraint. The Price Commission and Pay Board were disbanded and the CLC took charge of the policy. The price and wage controls were relaxed, with Tier I firms no longer being required to give notice of wage and price changes, and relative wages becoming an important factor. During Phase II food prices increased at almost twice the rate of the consumer price index and this difference increased during Phase III. At the same time energy costs rose worldwide and there was strong pressure on costs. Phase III lasted five months during which wholesale prices rose by 21.7 per cent. Mounting political pressure led to a 60-day freeze from June 1973. External factors caused prices to continue rising so public support rapidly declined. Phase IV followed the end of the freeze in August 1973, and allowed dollar-for-dollar costs to be passed on. Controls were removed from industries selectively from October, following a pledge to restrain wages and prices in the future. The final controls ended in April 1974.

Whether the controls, taken as a whole were effective is hard to judge. Price inflation and unemployment fell during 1971–2 under Phase I and Phase II and the increase in inflation in 1973–4 can be blamed on food and energy price increases, which reflected external influences. It is certainly true that initially they were a popular measure and the longer they continued the less support they received. Reid (1981) concluded that the controls did not effect the rate of wage change in Phase II, since the target increase would have occurred without the controls. However, in the case of Phase IV he found that wages were affected by the controls even though the actual rate of wage increase exceeded the 5.5 per cent target. Blinder and Newton (1981) found that while the controls had a temporary effect on prices, which the price explosion in 1974 cancelled, they increased the variance of inflation.

Pay and Price Standards 1978–82

When President Carter took office in 1977 inflation was accelerating sharply and there was a large budget deficit. The administration repeatedly rejected the use of controls and attempted to control monetary expansion. This led to higher interest rates and a fall in the international value of the dollar. Early in 1978 unions were asked to moderate their wage claims and companies to reduce their rate of price increases. This seemed to have no effect. By September the consumer price index had risen 6.7 per cent in 1978 compared to 6.8 per cent in the whole of 1977. President Carter reacted in October 1978 with the announcement of 'voluntary' standards for pay and price increases to be administered by the Council on Wage and Price Stability (CWPS). Price increases were to be limited to the previous actual percentage increase less one half of one per cent. If this was not possible because of cost increases profit margins were to be held at the average level of the best two of the last three years. In practice the CWPS used the profit margin as the criterion for increases. The pay limit applied to units of employees instead of individual workers and permitted a 7 per cent increase in wages and fringe benefits, net of overtime pay. Various exemptions, favouring workers, covered existing agreements, piece-rate schemes and low pay. Also linked with these proposals was a 'real wage insurance' scheme whereby groups which accepted wage rises of up to 7 per cent would benefit from tax credits if inflation exceeded 7 per cent. This is discussed in section 3.6 of Chapter 3. The real wage insurance scheme was rejected by Congress and so never came into effect. During 1979 oil prices rose, productivity fell and prices continued to rise and by October the standards appeared to be failing. Meyer (1980) however, concludes that, for the first year, while the actual increase in wages was more than 7 per cent, much of the excess can be explained by the permitted exemptions. President Carter decided that action was needed and he both tightened monetary policy and reorganised the controls. A new advisory committee with business, union and public members was set up in an attempt to involve unions. A revised pay standard of 8.5 per cent was announced in January 1980 and various measures to reduce government expenditure and consumer credit followed. Interest rates fell back sharply and the country entered a recession in the run up to the presidential election. All wage and price controls ended with the victory of Ronald Reagan and the introduction of supply-side policies.

1.5   NEW ZEALAND

The New Zealand economy differs from that of the UK and USA in size, growth and the degree of intervention in the labour market. In 1950 the labour force was 736 000 and this rose to 1 400 000 in 1985, an increase of 90 per cent over this period. Details of economic events in New Zealand are given in the various issues of the *New Zealand Official Yearbook*, the OECD reports on the country and the *Reserve Bank of New Zealand Bulletin*. Here we will examine the history of price controls and the method of wage determination before turning to incomes policies.

The Background to Price Controls

During the Second World War and immediately after, all prices were controlled with subsidies applying to many items including clothing, dairy produce and wheat. In 1947 the Control of Prices Act set up the Price Tribunal to fix prices and to investigate complaints from consumers. Between 1948 and 1968 there was a gradual relaxation of controls, with items such as fish, cake, jewellery and cosmetics being freed by the early fifties while 'basic' products like bread, butter, eggs and flour were still being controlled (and subsidised) as late as 1965. The method of control changed in 1955 to a 'positive list' approach. That is, only products named on the positive list were controlled. Two categories of goods were identified: the basic products, believed to be important items in the household budget, and products where there was a worry that retailers might exploit their monopoly power. This latter category arose for two reasons: the small domestic market and import restrictions. The small domestic market meant that for many products there were only one or two main manufacturers so that there was the possibility of excessive profits.

Customs tariffs have been used in New Zealand since the 1840s to protect domestic producers from unfair competition and dumping, and also to conserve foreign exchange. During the Second World War import licensing was used to ensure that overseas funds would be available to purchase essential imports. This continued after the war but in the 1950s the National Government reduced the scope of the licensing scheme until, by 1957, licensed private imports accounted for only 13 per cent of all private imports. A balance of payments crisis in 1957, which coincided with the election of a Labour Government, led to a reversal of this policy and new import controls were imposed. Priority was given to food imports and to raw materials for factories. In the sixties and seventies the scope of the licensing scheme was gradually reduced so that by 1979 approximately 25 per cent of private imports were licensed. New import licensing policies were introduced in 1979 to increase New Zealand's export competitiveness. These included a tendering scheme for some import licences and were followed in 1984 by proposals to move gradually to a tariff-based system.

The whole complex of import and price controls was accepted by both employers and employees in the fifties and early sixties for two main reasons. First, the high unemployment of the thirties meant that there was a strong determination to keep the full employment of the immediate postwar era. Secondly, since most of New Zealand's foreign currency was earned from agricultural exports, where prices are determined on the world market, the politically powerful farming lobby was able to stress the need to keep domestic costs low in the interests of national prosperity.

Wage Determination

The system of wage determination has been described in detail by Boston (1984), Mardle (1968) and Ledingham (1973) as well as in the wages section of the *New Zealand Official Yearbook* (1984) and earlier. Hughes and Silverstone (1980) provide a brief summary of wages policy in the 1970s. In 1894 the Industrial Conciliation and Arbitration Act set up the Court of Arbitration to be the final court of settlement in wage disputes. The Court is independent of the government. There is therefore a long history of legal involvement in wage determination. The process of reaching a settlement is for either workers or employers to frame a wage claim and convey this to the other party. If this is not fully accepted within a short time a 'dispute' is said to exist and a Council of Conciliation is set up by the Supreme Court to hear the dispute. The Council has a Conciliation Commissioner as chairman and an equal number of assessors appointed by employers and employees. The Council attempts to reach a full or partial agreement and the terms of the agreement are referred to the Court of Arbitration for approval or, in the absence of agreement, for compulsory arbitration. Any wage rates approved by the Court are minima which are then used by workers and employers as the basis for negotiations on actual rates of pay. Employers may be willing to pay above-award rates in exchange for concessions by the local workforce. Workers are happy to accept low awards from the Court in the knowledge that actual rates will be higher. The result of all this is that, as Mardle (1968) says, there is genuine collective bargaining and the compulsory arbitration aspect is not important.

When the Court reaches a decision or approves an agreement this can have important repercussions on other settlements. Up to the late 1960s two instruments were available to the Court for the specific purpose of influencing the general climate of negotiations. These were standard wage pronouncements (SWP) and general wage orders (GWO). Between 1919 and 1952, seven SWPs were made. These indicate the standard rates for unskilled, semi-skilled and skilled adult male workers that will be taken into account by the Court in future awards. Because both employers and employees were unhappy about the operation of

SWPs, none were made after 1952. A GWO can be issued by the Court on the Courts own initiative or in response to a request from employers or employees. It has the effect of increasing all minimum rates of pay from a specified date by either a fixed amount or a stated percentage. In determining the size of a GWO the Court hears comments from interested parties and must take into account changes in retail prices, economic conditions in New Zealand, productivity and output changes, and anything else it decides is relevant. According to Mardle (1968) applications for a GWO are made when real wages fall and so the unions regard the GWO as a means of adjusting wages for price increases.

Incomes Policy

In view of the amount of intervention by the government in price setting and by the Court of Arbitration in wage determination it might appear that there would be no need for incomes policies in New Zealand. However, after the 19.45 per cent devaluation of the New Zealand dollar in November 1967, at a time when there were very few price controls and inflation had increased from 3.2 per cent in the year to March 1967 to 6.2 per cent in the year to March 1968, the government announced a two-month price freeze from June 1968 together with a nil GWO. The previous GWO had been for 2.5 per cent in December 1966. Since then consumer prices had risen by 7.6 per cent. The nil GWO was a shock to the unions and, after pressure from both employers and unions, a restricted 5 per cent GWO was announced from August 1968. According to Rose (1972) the Court had seemed to misunderstand its role and so unions and employers combined to change the rules of the wage determination process, leading to larger wage increases over the next few years. While this explanation may be correct, it is important to realise that between 1968 and 1971 prices rose by 23 per cent in New Zealand, 23 per cent in the United Kingdom, 21 per cent in Japan and 16 per cent in the United States. In view of this a more general explanation of why inflation occurred is needed.

Following the price freeze in mid-1968 there was a return to free collective bargaining and a National Development Conference was held which set as the overall target an average growth rate of real gross national product of 4.5 per cent for the next decade. In April 1970 a voluntary scheme for the 'early warning' notification of price increases was introduced in an attempt to restrain prices. Inflation continued to increase, being 4.3 per cent in 1968, 4.9 per cent in 1969 and 5.5 per cent in the first nine months of 1970. A two-month price freeze was announced in November 1970, and extended to February 1971. There was a 3 per cent GWO in November 1970 and in March 1971 the Stabilization of Remuneration Act was passed which restricted wage increases to below 7 per cent. A price justification scheme started in February 1971 covering 110 items for which price increases had to be notified to the Department of Trade and Industry to allow objections to be raised. Another wage and price freeze applied for two months from February 1972 and was followed by a period of free bargaining after the election of a Labour government in December 1972. However, inflation rose in 1973 and the balance of payments deteriorated so the government introduced the Economic Stabilization Regulations 1973 in December to restrict wage increases by requiring a 12-month interval between settlements.

The period 1975–85 was notable for the almost continuous price restrictions, with price freezes in August 1976, June 1982 and July 1984 and little scope for increases at other times. Wages were determined by 'free' collective bargaining but with low maximum increases between 1975 and 1977. Wage freezes occurred in March 1977 and from June 1982 to 1985. The balance of payments current account was always in deficit. Unemployment increased over this period. In 1974 fewer than 1000 were unemployed representing less than 1 per cent of the workforce. By 1980 this had increased to 2.3 per cent and by 1984 to 4.7 per cent.

The election of the Labour government in July 1984 resulted in a general change in economic policy. There was an immediate 20 per cent devaluation of the New Zealand dollar followed in December 1984 by the freeing of exchange controls. Interest rates which had previously been regulated were also freed. The New Zealand dollar was floated from March 1985. The implications that these policies have for wage and price determination remain to be seen.

1.6 AUSTRALIA

While superficially Australia differs from the United Kingdom and the United States in having a small population (around 15 million in 1980) for a large area (32 times greater than the United Kingdom or approximately the same size as the United States excluding Alaska) it exhibits many of the characteristics of other industrial economies. For a comprehensive review of the Australian economy see Caves and Krause (1984). Over the past 40 years there have been some important changes.

In the early 1950s over 80 per cent of exports came from the rural sector while by 1980 this had dropped to 40 per cent. Exports of minerals rose from 6 per cent to 37 per cent, and of manufactured goods from around 3 per cent to 20 per cent of total exports over this period. The government sector is also important with government ownership of enterprises in transport (rail, air and local), electricity, coal, telecommunications, banking and broadcasting, as well as providing the usual state and local government services. Employment by the government accounted for 30 per cent of wage and salary earners in 1981 so that, as in the United Kingdom, the government has an important influence on remuneration rates. The Australian dollar was linked to the pound sterling until 1971, the American dollar from 1971–4 and a mixed currency basket from 1974–6. Since 1976 there has been a managed float.

The Wage-Determination Process

The method of determining wages in Australia has some similarities to that of New Zealand described above. For a detailed discussion see Isaac (1972) and Lansbury (1978). In 1904 the Commonwealth Court of Conciliation and Arbitration was set up to prevent and to settle industrial disputes by providing a means of compulsory arbitration. At this time the unions were relatively weak and by registering with the Court they obtained certain rights, including recognition by employers. A system of federal and state tribunals developed.

During the 1930's depression the employers applied to the Court for a reduction in the basic wage which was originally fixed in 1907 and had been increased each quarter with cost-of-living adjustments. The Court accepted the employers' claim that the basic wage was too high in view of the depression and the basic wage was reduced by 10 per cent. This established the precedent that the Court had to take account of the state of the national economy when making decisions about the basic wage rate.

After the Second World War the Court tried various methods of dealing with the problem of deciding both industry's capacity to pay and the desired level of wage adjustments. In 1956 the Court was reorganised into two structures: the Commonwealth Industrial Court to consider judicial matters and the Commonwealth Conciliation and Arbitration Commission to deal with problems of individual industries.

Following the Korean War and the high inflation it generated (40 per cent between 1950 and 1952) automatic cost of living adjustments were discontinued because of the desire to take the ability of employers to pay as an important element in wage determination. From 1956 the national basic wage was reviewed annually and, separately, margins were examined at the request of the unions. By 1965 it was agreed to hold joint meetings to fix both parts of wages. The basic wage was abandoned in 1967 when a total award for each job class was determined. From then the Commission became able to raise all wages by a common percentage, by the same cash amount or by different amounts. Each year a national wage was determined and then the problems of particular industries were dealt with by the Commissioners. By the late 1960s the differences between the award rates and the actual wages paid had become a serious problem. Since the Commission was making awards it believed to be reasonable from consideration of productivity changes, the higher settlements were inflationary. There were four sources of wage increase by 1970: (i) national wage awards applying to everyone (ii) formal and informal agreements at firm and industry level above the national award standards (iii) quasi-awards at industry level made by conciliation, reflecting union power and (iv) arbitration awards at firm and industry level matching rises in (ii) and (iii) for weak unions in the interests of 'wage justice'. The Commission tried to make award wages more realistic in the early 1970s with little success in reducing the additions to them. In 1973 the newly elected Labour government attempted to promote free collective bargaining with the result of high settlements, rising inflation and increasing unemployment. At the time of the 1974 national wage case the federal government and the Australian Council of Trade Unions both argued for full indexation of wages to prices but this was rejected.

Wage Controls

The 1975 national wage case marked a turning point in the wage determination. The federal government had argued for 'plateau' indexation which is a full percentage increase in all wages up to average weekly earnings and a flat amount increase above that level. The Commission agreed to full indexation in March 1975 but retained the right to vary the amount of the indexation at the end of each quarter. Also, each year an extra increase would be awarded on account of national productivity increases. Plowman (1981) describes the details. This ruling by the Commission was interpreted as an incomes policy by, for example, Dabscheck (1975). In the year to December 1974 average earnings had increased by 27.7 per cent, while prices, in the year to

March 1975 had risen by 17.6 per cent. Company profits had been squeezed and unemployment was at a postwar high of 4.6 per cent. The Commission saw as its main function the need to end the decline in economic activity and the fall in profitability which it saw as resulting from high wage settlements. In future only a single tier of wage determination would apply and this would be indexed wage increases from the Commission. Special cases for increases could be made for changes in the nature or conditions of work and also for catch-up movements. The federal government agreed to ask the Prices Justification Tribunal (see below) to disallow wage increases in excess of indexation as an argument for price increases.

Following the adoption of the new policy in April 1975, indexation was applied in full for the next few months. However, with the change of government at the end of 1975 the commitment to indexation was under threat since the Fraser government regarded it as inflationary. In 1976 the federal government argued for zero indexation and as a compromise the Commission agreed to plateau indexation. By the end of 1976 inflation was below 10 per cent. Throughout 1977 the Commission awarded less than full indexation, partly in the hope of tax concessions by the government (see Dabscheck, 1978). In April 1977 a three-month price–wage freeze was announced by the Prime Minister, with the intention of delaying further indexation awards. The Prices Justification Tribunal was instructed to defer price applications for this period. The unions rejected the need for a freeze. When the Commission met in May it announced that the price freeze was outside its control and made a partial indexation award which excluded the estimated 0.4 per cent of inflation due to devaluation.

As partial indexation continued it became increasingly unpopular with the unions, employers and the federal government. At the June 1978 national wage case the Commission threatened to scrap it and instead switched to six-monthly full indexation. Plateau indexation was formally abandoned. By this time inflation was below 8 per cent. For 1979 partial indexation was granted and increasing emphasis was placed on extra payments because of changes in 'work value' that is, in the nature of the work, skill and responsibility required or in the conditions under which work is performed. There was a trend towards decentralised wage determination which continued through 1980 when again only partial indexation was awarded.

The Commission abandoned indexation in July 1981 after disagreements between unions, which had been using industrial action to press their claims for full indexation, and employers, who wanted productivity-linked awards. Eventually an agreement was reached in the metal industry in December 1981 giving an increase in wages and a reduction in hours, together with a commitment to no further claims within twelve months. This led to a large number of similar claims, on a case by case basis, which resulted in high settlements. Unemployment rose from 6 per cent in 1981 to 10 per cent by 1983.

In December 1982 a special Premiers Conference agreed to a freeze on public sector wages for six months in New South Wales, Victoria and South Australia and twelve months elsewhere, with efforts to obtain a similar pause in the private sector. The opposition Labour Party agreed a Statement of Accord on economic policy with the Australian Council of Trade Unions in February 1983. This took on importance in the following month when the Labour Party, headed by Mr Hawke, won the federal election. The Australian dollar was devalued by 10 per cent. A national economic summit conference was held in April and resulted in an agreement to return to centralised wage fixing and to set up a prices surveillance authority. In September 1983 the return to half-yearly indexation was confirmed in the decision on the national wage case and the pay pause ended.

The first six months of 1984 resulted in a fall in the consumer price index of 0.2 per cent and no wage case was heard. A joint union/government working party agreed on tax cuts as part of the Accord and these were announced in the August budget. However, in the second half of 1984 wage drift (the difference between the increase in basic wages and total earnings) reappeared and the future success of wage restraint was in doubt. In July 1985 agreement was reached between the unions and the federal government for support for full indexation in the 1985 national wage case in return for 2 per cent discount on wage indexation in 1986.

Price Controls

There were no methods available to the government in Australia for controlling prices before 1973. In that year the Labour government asked for powers to control prices and incomes but this was rejected in a referendum. Instead the Prices Justification Tribunal (PJT) was set up in August 1973 with the job of deciding whether price increases by companies were justified. The early history of the PJT is described by Dabscheck (1977) and Fels (1981). The act setting up the PJT did not give any criteria for evaluating proposed price increases. Any company with a turnover of $20 million or more was required to advise the PJT of their intention to raise their prices. Within 21 days of receiving this notification the PJT had either to accept the application or to recommend a lower price. If a price could not be agreed between the company and the PJT a public enquiry would be held which reported to the Prime Minister. Increasing prices without PJT approval or before the report of the public enquiry was published was not in fact punishable and the only sanction was bad publicity. The decisions of the PJT were generally accepted by companies.

Dabscheck (1977) explains that the PJT adopted a hard line in keeping prices down below the level they would otherwise have been in the period up to November 1974. This was achieved by delaying increases through holding public enquiries and also by forcing companies to absorb some costs. The economy was booming from early 1973 till mid-1974 but then went into a down-swing with unemployment increasing from 1.5 per cent in 1973 to 4 per cent by December 1974. Because of the down-turn and also a request from the Prime Minister, Mr Whitlam, asking the PJT to take account of the need to stimulate private investment and to restore profit levels, policy changed in November 1974. The PJT held fewer public enquiries, the pressure on firms to absorb cost increases declined, the processing of price notifications was speeded up and the PJT indicated the grounds on which it was prepared to accept price increases.

By April 1975, when wage indexation was introduced, the PJT was approving high price increases which resulted in high wage increases and so on. Dabscheck (1977) argues that any apparent success of the PJT between 1974 and 1976 was due to the higher level of unemployment over this period. There was evidence that by 1976 the PJT was worsening inflation. Norman (1976) found that because of the depression some prices sanctioned by the PJT were too high and also in other cases the approval of the PJT meant that increased prices were readily accepted. The change of government after the December 1975 elections affected the role of the PJT. The new Coalition government had intended to abolish the PJT but retained it in an attempt to get the support of the unions for wage restraint. In December 1976 there were a number of changes in the PJT regulations (see Plowman (1981) for details) exempting from control firms in 'strongly competitive markets', retail companies and small subsidiary companies. The number of notifications of price increases to the PJT declined by half from 1976 to 1977 and again by half from 1977 to 1978. The PJT was further limited in June 1978 by a ministerial request to exempt nearly all companies from notifying proposed price increases: the only companies still covered were those of which, following a public enquiry, the PJT required notification. By October 1978 only the wool-broking and petroleum product areas were in this category. At this time the role of the PJT was described by the government as 'price surveillance' rather than price control. The effects of the world recession had reduced the need for the PJT and in April 1981 the Prime Minister, Mr Fraser, announced its abolition. However, two months later the Petroleum Products Pricing Authority was set up to conduct enquiries in relation to prices of the petroleum products industry and to report to the Treasurer.

It is difficult to see how the PJT could have had much effect beyond the first year or so. Mitchell (1984) points out that widespread shortages did not occur so any effect must have been minimal. Chapman and Junor (1981) also found the effect of the PJT to be small.

The original Accord proposal in February 1983 included a statement that prices should be regulated (see Mulvey, 1984) but no steps were taken to do so until December 1983, when, after union complaints legislation to set up the Prices Surveillance Authority (PSA) was passed. The PSA started operation in March 1984 and put the petroleum industry prices and postal and telecommunications charges under surveillance. A public enquiry into the principles and practices of pricing petroleum products was held by the PSA and the results accepted by the government. The range of products covered by the PSA was gradually extended to include wholesale prices of beer, cigarettes, float glass and concrete roofing tiles in December 1984 and tea, coffee and fruit juices by March 1985. Whether controlling prices of this rather limited list of products will have any effect on inflation remains to be seen.

1.7 OTHER COUNTRIES

There are a number of studies which cover the history of incomes policies in Western Europe. For the postwar period to 1970, Ulman and Flanagan (1971) review the experience of the United Kingdom, the Netherlands, Sweden, Denmark, France, Western Germany and Italy. Addison (1981) covers the period up to 1980 in Austria, Finland, France, Western Germany, Ireland, the Netherlands and Norway. The more recent history of Austria, the Netherlands, Norway, Western Germany, Sweden, the United Kingdom, Denmark, Italy and France is discussed in Flanagan, Soskice and Ulman (1983). Much useful background information on economic policy for these countries is presented in Krause and Salant (1977) and Lovett (1982).

Further details on incomes policies for particular countries are given in Edgren, Faxen and Odhner (1973) for Sweden, Addison (1979) for Finland, Ireland and Norway, Albeda (1985) for the Netherlands, Reid (1979) for Canada, Cohen (1974) for Nigeria, ILO (1972) for Kenya and Palekar (1962) and Fonseca (1975) for India. Smith (1969) reviews wages policies for underdeveloped countries in general, and Adam (1982) discusses their role in Eastern Europe.

1.8 CONCLUSIONS

From the widespread experience of wage and price controls in different countries over different historical periods it is possible to identify what might be termed a 'conventional incomes policy'. This starts with a statement by the government that targets are to be set for future wage and price increases. The government then attempts to get support from employers' and workers' representatives. Next some form of monitoring body is set up to investigate excessive increases and pleas for exemption. The general experience of these conventional incomes policies seems to be that they are effective for a short while and then, because of pressures to relax the controls, the policies are either abandoned completely or are modified to deal with new circumstances. At first sight this might suggest that the controls generally fail. However, such a conclusion, based on a casual examination of historical evidence, is likely to be unreliable. The important point is that the effectiveness of an incomes policy can only be determined by comparing what actually happened with what would have happened in the absence of the controls. In the next chapter we examine ways in which conventional incomes policies might be assessed.

2 Conventional Incomes Policies

2.1 ASSESSING THE IMPACT OF INCOMES POLICIES

We saw in Chapter 1 that various western governments have attempted, by means of incomes policies, to influence the way in which wages and prices change. In this chapter, in sections 2.1–2.3 we first consider how the effects of an incomes policy might be determined. Theories of wage and price determination are presented and the empirical evidence relating to them is reviewed in sections 2.4–2.8. In section 2.9 the microeconomic implications of an incomes policy are discussed and in section 2.10 the political rationale for an incomes policy is considered. A summary of our conclusions is presented in section 2.11.

In order to assess the impact of an incomes policy on the macroeconomic variables of interest (such as wages or prices), a model is needed which explains how these variables are determined in the absence of the incomes policy. This model is used to predict the values of the variables during the period of the incomes policy, providing the *base run*. Next the model is modified to make allowance for the imposition of the incomes policy and new predictions are made. The differences between these and the base run reflect the effects of the incomes policy.

This procedure can be followed in two different ways. One method is to use economic theory to formulate behavioural or structural equations which explain the chosen economic variables. The second approach is to go directly to the reduced form and use this to predict the variables of interest. The reduced form is the solution of the economic model in which the endogenous variables (those variables explained by the model) are expressed in terms of exogenous variables (those variables determined outside the model) and lagged endogenous variables.

We now consider both of these approaches.

2.2 THE BEHAVIOURAL APPROACH

The basis of this approach is to specify, in the absence of an incomes policy, the behavioural or structural equations of the model, that is the equations which reflect the underlying economic theory. To illustrate this, consider the following simple model of an economy:

$$Y = C + I + G \tag{2.1}$$

$$C = \delta Y + (1 - \gamma) C_{-1} + u_1 \tag{2.2}$$

$$I = \beta(Y - Y_{-1}) + u_2 \tag{2.3}$$

$$p = \alpha(Y - \overline{Y}) + u_3 \tag{2.4}$$

where Y is real income

p is the rate of inflation

C is real consumption

$\overline{Y}$ is full employment income (assumed to be constant)

I is real investment

G is real government expenditure (assumed exogenous)

u_1, u_2 and u_3 are random error terms

α, β, γ and δ are constants and a negative subscript indicates a lag.

Equation (2.1) is the familiar national income identity for a closed economy and (2.2) is a fairly standard consumption function in which consumption depends on current disposable income and past consumption. One interpretation of (2.2) is the permanent income hypothesis with permanent income represented by past income. Investment is determined by an accelerator mechanism (2.3) and (2.4) is a naïve Phillips curve. In this model all the equations are linear and there is no feedback between inflation and the real variables so that simultaneity is restricted to (2.1)–(2.3) with (2.4) then giving inflation. There are four endogenous variables (Y, C, I and p) explained by two exogenous variables ($G, \overline{Y}$) and two lagged endogenous variables (C_{-1}, Y_{-1}). This model is intentionally simple. To make it realistic would require further equations to explain how a modern economy works.

In practice, when researchers are studying the effects of incomes policies they concentrate on the price and/or wage equations rather than specifying a complete macroeconomic model. Thus the equations of interest might be:

$$w = f(X_1 X_2 \ldots X_n) \tag{2.5}$$

$$p = g(Z_1 Z_2 \ldots Z_m) \tag{2.6}$$

where w and p are the rates of change of nominal wages and prices respectively, and the X_i and Z_i are economic variables. Typically these include the unemployment rate, price expectations and productivity growth, with some variables occurring in both equations. Also, one of the X variables might be p and one of the Z variables w, giving a simultaneous determination of wages and prices. Assuming for simplicity that (2.5) and (2.6) are linear, in the absence of incomes policies we can write

$$w = \alpha_0 + \alpha_1 X_1 + \alpha_2 X_2 + \ldots + u_1 \tag{2.7}$$

$$p = \beta_0 + \beta_1 Z_1 + \beta_2 Z_2 + \ldots + u_2 \tag{2.8}$$

where the α_i and β_i are constants and u_1 and u_2 are random error terms.

Next the researcher must decide how to model the influence of incomes policies on wages and prices. We consider two possibilities. The first is to use dummy variables. That is, a new variable is introduced which takes the value of unity when an incomes policy is in operation and zero otherwise. For example in the case of (2.7) we write

$$w = \alpha_0 + \gamma D + \alpha_1 X_1 + \alpha_2 X_2 + \ldots + u_1 \tag{2.9}$$

where D is the dummy variable.

The effect of introducing D is that in the absence of the incomes policy (when $D = 0$) (2.9) is the same as (2.7) but during the incomes policy (when $D = 1$) there is an extra intercept term γ in (2.9). The impact of the incomes policy on wages can then be assessed by estimating the value of γ and testing whether it is significantly negative (since the incomes policy is expected to reduce wage inflation). In this case the effect of the incomes policy is to shift the relationship between w and $X_1 \ldots X_n$ by a constant amount γ since the dummy variable is added to (2.7). Perry (1970) and Eckstein and Brinner (1972) follow this approach.

The use of additive dummy variables, as in (2.9), to model incomes policies implicitly assumes that the incomes policies do not change the way in which the variables X_1, X_2, ... effect wages. That is, α_1, α_2, ... remain invariant to the policies. This assumption may be invalid. For example, suppose X_1 is the variable p. One of the usual reasons for imposing an incomes policy (as we saw in Chapter 1) is to break the link between w and p. If, in the absence of an incomes policy α_1 is, say, 1.0, the effect of the policy might be to change α_1 to 0.5 with the result that for any given value of p, the wage change, w, is proportionately smaller.

This possibility can be incorporated by introducing both additive (or intercept) dummies and also slope (or multiplicative) dummies. For example, the wage equation (2.7) could be written

$$w = \delta_0 + \gamma_0 D + (\delta_1 + \gamma_1 D)X_1 + (\delta_2 + \gamma_2 D)X_2 + \ldots + u_1 \qquad (2.10)$$

where the intercept term α_0 has been replaced by

$$\delta_0 + \gamma_0 D, \quad \alpha_1 \text{ by } \quad \delta_1 + \gamma_1 D, \text{ etc.}$$

In the absence of an incomes policy $D = 0$ so that (2.10) becomes

$$w = \delta_0 + \delta_1 X_1 + \delta_2 X_2 + \ldots + u_1 \qquad (2.11)$$

while with an incomes policy $D = 1$ so that (2.10) becomes

$$w = \delta_0 + \gamma_0 + (\delta_1 + \gamma_1)X_1 + (\delta_2 + \gamma_2)X_2 + \ldots + u_1 \qquad (2.12)$$

Comparing (2.11) and (2.12) the effects of the incomes policy are γ_0, γ_1, γ_2, ... This use of dummy variables can be further generalised to allow for several incomes policies of different forms and strengths. In principle a new dummy variable can be introduced for each postulated form of incomes policy. Furthermore, a wide variety of effects, such as whether the impact is temporary or permanent, or whether the announcement of a future incomes policy has any immediate impact, can be modelled by different dummy variables. Thus, for example, the recent work of Henry and Ormerod (1978) and Henry (1981) employ nine incomes policy dummy variables: five to represent the impact of the operation of different types of incomes policies and four to represent possible 'catch-up' periods following the relaxation of the policies. However, while the flexibility of dummy variables has its attractions, their introduction is frequently limited by the number of observations available on the data. Notice that (2.10) has twice as many unknown parameters as (2.7).

The second approach to measuring the impact of incomes policies is to split the available data into those periods when incomes policies are in operation (policy-on) and those when there are no incomes policies (policy-off). A theoretical model, such as (2.7), is estimated for each period and the resulting coefficients are compared to see if the incomes policies have any effect. This method was used by Lipsey and Parkin (1970) and can be interpreted as a generalisation of using dummy variables since it is equivalent to estimating (2.11) and (2.12) but now allowing the error term to have different properties in the policy-on and policy-off periods. One limitation of the Lipsey–Parkin procedure is that it requires the assumption that the various types of incomes policy experienced can be treated as having the same quantitative effect.

2.3 THE REDUCED FORM APPROACH

The alternative to the behavioural approach is to go directly to the reduced form of a model and to use that to examine the effects of incomes policies on appropriate variables. To illustrate this consider the following model based on (2.7) and (2.8)

$$w = \alpha_0 + \alpha_1 p + \alpha_2 X_2 + u_1 \qquad (2.13)$$

$$p = \beta_0 + \beta_1 w + \beta_2 Z_2 + u_2 \qquad (2.14)$$

where the endogenous variables w and p are explained by X_2 (say the deviation of output from its trend value) and Z_2 (say the growth of productivity). The reduced form can be obtained by substituting from (2.14) for p into (2.13) which gives

$$w = \alpha_0 + \alpha_1 (\beta_0 + \beta_1 w + \beta_2 Z_2 + u_2) + \alpha_2 X_2 + u_1$$

or, by re-arranging,

$$w = \frac{1}{(1 - \alpha_1 \beta_1)} (\alpha_0 + \alpha_1 \beta_0 + \alpha_1 \beta_2 Z_2 + \alpha_2 X_2 + \alpha_1 u_2 + u_1) \qquad (2.15)$$

and similarly, by substituting from (2.13) for w into (2.14),

$$p = \frac{1}{(1 - \alpha_1 \beta_1)} (\beta_0 + \alpha_0 \beta_1 + \alpha_2 \beta_1 X_2 + \beta_2 Z_2 + \beta_1 u_1 + u_2) \qquad (2.16)$$

In both (2.15) and (2.16) an endogenous variable is explained by the pre-determined variables X_2 and Z_2. More generally, the reduced form of any model expresses each endogenous variable in terms of all the pre-determined variables (that is, exogenous and lagged endogenous variables). Therefore it is not necessary to go through the process of solving the equations explicitly since with the model (2.13) and (2.14) the endogenous variables are w and p and the pre-determined variables are X_2 and Z_2 so the reduced form can be written

$$w = f_1(X_2, Z_2) \qquad (2.17)$$

$$p = f_2(X_2, Z_2) \qquad (2.18)$$

The reduced form equations can be estimated for the variables of interest and the effect of incomes policies could be modelled by introducing intercept and/or slope dummy variables as explained in the previous section. Minford and Brech (1981) and Darby (1976) use this approach to explain the rate of inflation by current and past changes in money stock.

The advantage of the reduced form approach is in its flexibility. The researcher can focus on one variable (inflation, say), and ignore other endogenous variables. However, this is at the cost of losing some of the benefits from a structural model. For example, with (2.13) and (2.14), economic theory might suggest that β_2 is negative so that the coefficient on Z_2 in (2.15) is expected to be negative since both α_1 and $1 - \alpha_1 \beta_1$ are expected to be positive. In contrast, there is no prior information on the signs of coefficients in (2.17) when it is considered independently of (2.13) and (2.14).

A variation on the reduced form approach is the time series method in which the variables of interest are represented by autoregressive moving average (or ARMA) models. Thus, for example the model for inflation might be

$$p_t = \alpha_0 + \alpha_1 p_{t-1} + \alpha_2 p_{t-2} + \beta_1 e_t + \beta_2 e_{t-1} \tag{2.19}$$

where e_t is a random disturbance. Here p is explained by its two most recent past values (and so the autoregressive part is of order 2) and by a moving average error of order 1. That is, (2.19) is said to be an ARMA (2, 1) model. Box and Jenkins (1970) showed that any variable with a constant mean, variance and covariances could be represented by an ARMA model of appropriate order. The details of how such a model is selected and estimated are explained by Pindyck and Rubinfeld (1981). For our purposes the important point is that the model is empirically determined, rather than being based on a theoretical structure.

The procedure for testing whether an incomes policy has an effect is to use data for a period with no incomes policy to estimate an appropriate ARMA model and to compare this model with one estimated when an incomes policy is in force. If the incomes policy has an effect then the parameters of the reduced form will change and the two estimated models will be different. A variation on this approach is to introduce dummy variables to represent the effects of incomes policy (see Box and Tiao, 1975, for an example).

A further method of evaluating the impact of incomes policies based on ARMA models is to use post-sample prediction. The estimated ARMA model (based on the period without an incomes policy) is used to predict the values of the variables of interest during the incomes policy. The closer the predictions are to the outcomes, the smaller is the effect of the incomes policy. Feige and Pearce (1976) and Hughes and Silverstone (1980) provide illustrations of this approach. The weakness of this method is that any change between the periods before and after the implementation of the incomes policy is attributed to the incomes policy when it may be due to other factors. For example changes in policy regime such as the switch from fixed to floating exchange rates in the UK or changes in administration in the USA should, a priori lead to changes in the appropriate ARMA and reduced form models. This leads us to prefer the use of structural models for assessing the impact of incomes policies. However, it should be pointed out that the use of reduced form models has been motivated by dissatisfaction with the performance of structural models (see, for example, Feige and Pearce, 1976). In order to understand why this dissatisfaction occurs we now turn to the specification of structural models of wage and price determination.

2.4 THE WAGE EQUATION

The wage equation attempts to explain the behaviour of either the level or rate of change of money wages. There is a considerable literature on this topic in which the explanatory variables include current and lagged values of the unemployment rate, the deviation of output from its trend value, the growth of productivity, the level (and changes in) the proportion of the labour force unionised, the number of strikes and proxies for the expected rate of inflation. However, it is possible to distinguish between two broad theoretical approaches to nominal wage determination, namely cost–push and optimisation. In the cost–push approach, wage and price changes are assumed to be determined independently of economic conditions within the economy. Agents are assumed to have monopoly power and to be able to engineer continuous wage or price increases irrespective of the market environment as defined by the demand for and supply of labour. Perhaps the most well-known empirical application of this approach is that of Hines (1964) who relates changes in nominal wages to the proportion and changes in the proportion of the labour force unionised. These two variables are proxies for union power.

The alternative approach to wage determination is based on the hypothesis that the aggregate rate of change of wages is the result of optimising behaviour by agents. There are three possibilities. First, if the labour market is competitive, real wages will be determined, given a contract period, by the interaction of the demand and supply curves for labour (see Aziaridis, 1975, and Chapter 5) which represent the aggregate outcomes of the constrained maximisation process of agents (see e.g. Gravelle and Rees, 1981). Secondly, if there is a 100 per cent unionisation of labour, real wages will be determined as the solution of the constrained optimisation decision of the union. The union acts as though it is maximising a utility function which represents the preferences of the members and union for income and leisure, subject to the demand function for labour services. In this approach the unions are given a key role in determining the level of real wages. However, unlike in the cost–push approach, unions are seen as rational agents who maximise their members' (and their own) interests subject to the demand constraint. Consequently the real wage outcome is not independent of economic factors but on the contrary crucially depends on them.

The third possibility is to model the aggregate labour market as a dual market embodying both a competitive and non-competitive (union) sector. In each sector wages are determined as explained above (see Minford and Brech, 1981). This dual labour market model borrows heavily from the economic development literature (see Lewis, 1954; Harris and Todaro, 1970).

From consideration of these broad approaches to wage determination it is clear that a rationale for incomes policies emerges if unions are seen as a source of exogenous wage–push or militancy. Incomes policies may be necessary to restrain such forces. However, it seems uncontroversial to recognise that unions do face a constraint in the form of the demand curve for labour so that they trade off higher wages against unemployment of their members. Consequently it is difficult to find credible a mechanism by which unions would wish (or could) engineer a continuing inflation. For instance suppose unions suddenly become more powerful and choose a higher real wage. In the absence of a market clearing competitive sector, this would emerge as a once-and-for-all wage increase. Continuing wage or price inflation from this source would require continuing increases in power or continually changing preferences in favour of a higher real wage. Such a scenario seems implausible. The observed behaviour of nominal wages on a time series basis would require a theory of cyclical surges in pushfulness or changes in preferences to explain the differing nominal wage changes of for instance 7 per cent in 1968 and 1977 and 20 per cent in 1974 in the UK. Given this, few economists seriously suggest that wage changes are independent of economic factors and so we do not give any further attention to pure cost–push models. Instead, we consider two models of the wage process in which the market environment effects wages. These are the augmented Phillips curve and the real wage resistance model, and they provide the basis for the majority of empirical tests of the impact of incomes policies.

2.5   THE AUGMENTED PHILLIPS CURVE

The 'old fashioned' Phillips curve, as outlined by Lipsey (1960), relates
the rate of change of money wages to the excess demand for labour.
Friedman (1968) and Phelps (1970), however, argue that agents do not
suffer from money illusion so that it is not money wages that agents are
concerned with but real wages. More precisely, it is *anticipated* real wages
which matter so that the Phillips curve is augmented to include price
expectations. Consequently we have

$$w = f\frac{(D-S)}{S} + p^e \tag{2.20}$$

where w is the rate of change of money wages, $(D-S)/S$ is the excess
demand for labour and p^e is the expected rate of inflation. The excess
demand for labour has been proxied by a variety of different variables in
empirical work such as linear or non-linear transformations of the
unemployment rate, past or present deviations of output from trend,
hoarded and hidden unemployment, lagged real wages and a time trend
(see Simler and Tella, 1968; Taylor, 1970; McCallum, 1975; 1976).

There are two theoretical rationales for the Phillips curve. If the
labour market is competitive then (2.20) represents the neo-classical
adjustment mechanism (see Hines, 1971). Alternatively if the labour
market is not competitive then the unions' bargaining strength is
assumed to vary with the degree of excess demand or supply of labour
(see Turnovsky, 1977).

Expected inflation is unobservable and has been proxied in a variety of
ways in empirical work. The usual approach is to employ a weighted
average of past inflation such as adaptive expectations. In its simplest
form the adaptive expectations mechanism is

$$p^e = p_{-1} \tag{2.21}$$

where p^e is the expected rate of inflation over the coming year and p_{-1} is
the actual rate of inflation over the past year.

We will now show that if price expectations are formed adaptively, as
in (2.21), in the absence of incomes policy but reduced by a constant
when an incomes policy is in operation, then the rate of wage inflation
will, *ceteris paribus*, be influenced by the incomes policy and hence so will
the behaviour of real output. To illustrate this point consider the

following model:

$$w = \alpha(Y - \overline{Y}) + p^e \qquad (2.22)$$

$$p = w \qquad (2.23)$$

$$p^e = p_{-1} - kD \qquad (2.24)$$

$$m = p + y \qquad (2.25)$$

where w is the rate of change of nominal wages, Y is the logarithm of real output (so that $y = Y - Y_{-1}$), $\overline{Y}$ is the logarithm of equilibrium real output, p is the rate of inflation, p^e is the expected rate of inflation, m is the rate of growth of the money supply and D is the dummy variable for the incomes policy. By substitution from (2.24) for p^e and (2.23) for w into (2.22), an equation in p and y is obtained and p is eliminated by using (2.25) to give

$$Y = \frac{1}{1 + \alpha} \{\alpha\overline{Y} + 2Y_{-1} - Y_{-2} + kD + m - m_{-1}\} \qquad (2.26)$$

This shows that the level of real output is, *ceteris paribus* higher with an incomes policy since the dummy variable D will be non-zero during its operation and k is a positive constant. The reason for this effect is because price expectations can be brought down independently of the previous inflation rate so that a given rate of inflation can be achieved at a lower cost in terms of transitory output loss with an incomes policy than in the absence of such a policy. This equation also illustrates how a contractionary monetary policy ($m < m_{-1}$) causes output to fall initially below its equilibrium value.

The above discussion implies that an incomes policy can have a useful role when adaptive expectations are present (see also Mayhew, 1981). However, if agents form their expectations adaptively in the absence of incomes policy, it is not clear what the justification is for assuming that they will revise their expectations mechanism when the incomes policy occurs.

A further problem with adaptive expectations is that at times of rising (or falling) inflation systematic errors will be made. In view of this other methods of expectation formation have been suggested. One important one is rational expectations in which it is assumed that the marginal costs and benefits of information gathering are such that agents will continue to process information until they obtain unbiased expectations (see, for example, Holden, Peel and Thompson, 1985). We will be returning to rational expectations later in the chapter. However, we note that, somewhat paradoxically, if expectations are formed rationally and if incomes policies affect the structural equations of the economy then incomes policies will also affect price expectations. For example, if the behavioural price equation is

$$p = \beta_1 X_{-1} - \beta_2 D + \beta_3 p^e \qquad (2.27)$$

where X is a vector of economic variables and D is an incomes policy dummy, then the rational expectation of inflation (which is obtained by setting $p = p^e$) if the incomes policy is anticipated is

$$p^e = \frac{1}{1-\beta_3} \{\beta_1 X_{-1} - \beta_2 D\} \qquad (2.28)$$

From this equation it is clear that the value of p^e depends on the effect of the incomes policy.

2.6 THE REAL WAGE RESISTANCE MODEL

The alternative to the augmented Phillips curve is the real wage resistance model of wage determination as suggested by Sargan (1964); Henry, Sawyer and Smith (1976) and Hicks (1974). The argument is that changes in nominal wages occur because unions attempt to secure a desired path of after-tax real wages in the bargaining process. A simple form of this hypothesis is

$$w = \alpha(R^a - R_{-1}) + p^e \qquad (2.29)$$

where R^a and R are the aspiration and actual real wages and α is a constant which depends on the retention ratio (or proportion of the wage retained after tax). The aspiration real wage is usually modelled as a time trend. However, this independence of aspirations from the real behaviour of the economy seems illogical and in the spirit of the cost–push approach to explaining inflation. In practice (2.29) is modified to include the unemployment rate as an extra variable. This can be interpreted as affecting either the speed of adjustment (α) or the aspiration real wage.

There is also a problem of observational equivalence between the real wage resistance hypothesis and the augmented Phillips curve (see Parkin, 1979). By observational equivalence is meant that each theory leads to an equation involving the same variables. For example, in the augmented Phillips curve (2.20) if the excess demand for labour depends on the lagged real wage (R_{-1}) and other variables (X) then we have

$$w = \alpha_0 + \alpha_1 R_{-1} + \alpha_2 X + p^e \tag{2.30}$$

Similarly if Z represents variables determining the aspiration real wage then (2.29) can be written

$$w = \beta_0 + \beta_1 Z + \beta_2 R_{-1} + p^e \tag{2.31}$$

Since the variables in X and Z may be the same there is no empirical way of distinguishing between (2.30) and (2.31). The real-wage resistance hypothesis does suggest a potential role for effective incomes policies in modifying the real wage aspirations of the labour force (see, for example, Artis, 1981). Whether this can be achieved will depend on the information set that agents possess and the precise mechanism for determining the aspiration real wage.

2.7 EMPIRICAL STUDIES

We now examine some of the empirical evidence on the effects of incomes policies on nominal wage change. Interestingly the main topic in the empirical literature is whether incomes policies have affected wages or prices, rather than the equally important consideration of the effects on output. We limit our coverage to four papers which we regard as the more important contributions in the literature. While these are all UK studies the methodology adopted has been used elsewhere (see Brunner and Meltzer, 1976, for example).

The first is by Lipsey and Parkin (1970) who use quarterly time series data for the UK for 1948(3)–1967(2). They identify four periods when incomes policies were in operation: the Labour Government's appeal to unions for wage restraint, 1948(3)–1950(3); Macmillan's 'price and wage plateau', 1956(1)–1956(4); Selwyn Lloyd's 'pay pause' and the National Incomes Commission 1961(3)–1964(3); and the Prices and Incomes Board 1964(4)–1968(2). Their approach is to estimate wage equation for (a) those periods with no incomes policy ('policy-off') (b) those periods with an incomes policy ('policy-on') and (c) the whole period. This assumes that the effects of the incomes policies are constant both within the lifetime of an incomes policy and between different incomes policies. Their empirical results for wage change are

Policy-off $\quad w = 6.672 - 2.372U + 0.457p + 0.136n \tag{2.32}$
$$\qquad\qquad (5.79) \quad (3.64) \quad (6.25) \quad (0.07)$$

$$R^2 = 0.856 \, DW = 1.231$$

Policy-on $w = 3.919 - 0.404U + 0.227p + 3.76n$ (2.33)
              (2.27)   (0.56)   (0.93)   (1.61)

$R^2 = 0.138 \; DW = 0.724$

Whole-period $w = 4.147 - 0.891U + 0.482p + 3.315n$ (2.34)
                 (4.26)   (1.77)   (5.76)   (2.09)

$R^2 = 0.616 \; DW = 0.742$

where w is the rate of change of weekly wage rates
    p is the rate of change of retail prices
    U is the percentage of the labour force unemployed measured as
       the average of the current and preceding two quarters
    n is the change in the percentage of the labour force unionised
    $t-$ values are in parentheses
    R^2 is the coefficient of determination
   DW is the Durbin–Watson statistic.

Lipsey and Parkin claim that these results are consistent with the hypothesis that incomes policies had an impact on the determination of nominal wage change. Comparing (2.32) and (2.33), of particular interest is the relationship between w and U when the other variables take their mean values over the data period. For the policy-off periods, this graph is steep with a slope of 2.372 while in policy-on periods the graph is much flatter with a slope of 0.404. The result is that the graph pivots on the unemployment rate of 1.8 per cent (see Figure 2.1). Thus for unemployment rates above 1.8 per cent wages rise more with an incomes policy in operation than when there is no incomes policy. This is explained by the suggestion that the 'norm' for the incomes policy becomes the minimum settlement rate even if demand conditions do not warrant such an increase.

A number of authors have questioned Lipsey and Parkin's results. Wallis (1971) points out that the Durbin–Watson statistics in (2.32)–(2.34) indicate autocorrelation so that the reported t-values are unreliable. Godfrey (1971) questions the assumption that inflation, unemployment and changes in trade union membership are exogenous, which is required for ordinary least squares estimates to be valid. He obtains very different estimates when he makes these variables endogenous and also allows for autocorrelated errors. Only inflation is significant and so Godfrey concludes that the Lipsey–Parkin model is inadequate. A further problem is the use of the actual rate of inflation for the expected rate of inflation. While this can be interpreted as the implicit

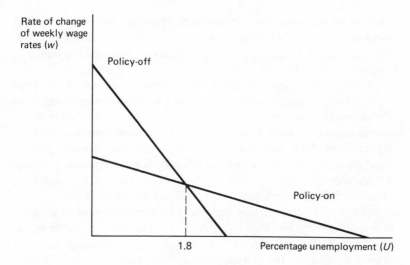

Figure 2.1

assumption of rational expectations which are unbiased so that

$$p = p^e + u \qquad (2.35)$$

where u is a random error, it introduces the extra complication of the errors in variable problem.

The second study of the impact of incomes policies on wages which we consider is by Henry and Ormerod (1978) who use quarterly data for the UK for the period 1960(1) to 1975(4). In the absence of incomes policies they assume that wages are determined by a real-wage aspiration model which takes the form

$$w = \alpha_0 + \alpha_1 U_{-1} + \alpha_2 p^e + \alpha_3 R_{-1} + \alpha_4 t \qquad (2.36)$$

where w is the rate of change of basic wage rates, U is the unemployment rate, p^e is the expected rate of retail price inflation, R is net real earnings, and t is a time trend. All the variables except t are in logarithmic form. Comparing (2.36) with (2.29) the aspiration real-wage is modelled by unemployment and the time trend.

Henry and Ormerod identify five periods of incomes policy: 1966(3)–1967(2), 1967(3)–1969(2), 1972(4)–1973(1), 1973(2)–1974(1) and 1975(3)–1977(2). These are represented by five additive dummy variables. The period following the end of an incomes policy is also of special concern to Henry and Ormerod. They introduce 'catch-up' dummies which allow wages to return to the path they would have been on had incomes policies never been introduced. These are for 1967(3)–1968(2), 1969(3)–1971(2), 1973(2)–1973(3) and 1974(2)–1975(1). The effect is that any wage increases foregone when a policy is in operation might be recovered when the policy ends.

For estimation purposes Henry and Ormerod use measures of the expected rate of inflation derived by the use of instrumental variables. Consequently (though not pointed out by Henry and Ormerod) one interpretation of their analysis is that they have assumed rational expectations. Unfortunately they do not use the incomes policies dummies as instruments, which is a mis-specification if incomes policies influence the structural wage equation since the rational expectation of inflation must also be influenced, in general, by incomes policies.

Because of autocorrelation Henry and Ormerod estimate their model in first differences. However this gives a constant term (the coefficient α_4 in (2.36)) which is insignificant and wrongly signed. Consequently they impose a value on the constant which, they argue, produces a more realistic value for the growth in desired real net earnings. The restriction is not rejected by the data.

Henry and Ormerod find that two incomes policy dummies are significant. In particular, the compulsory freeze of 1972(4)–1973(1) has a significantly negative impact on wage change. However, the catch-up dummy following this period of incomes policy is also significantly different from zero with a positive coefficient similar in size to that on the incomes policy dummy. Consequently Henry and Ormerod's work appears to provide evidence that this incomes policy constrained money wage increases when it operated, but in the period immediately following the policy money wage rates accelerated to compensate fully for the losses during the incomes policy.

There are a number of reasons to be sceptical of Henry and Ormerod's empirical findings. First the coefficient on expected inflation never takes a value in excess of 0.29 and is always significantly different from one. This implies a substantial degree of money illusion. We find this interpretation unsatisfactory and consequently suggest that it is evidence of a mis-specification of the equation. As we mentioned earlier this could in part be due to the omission of the incomes policy and catch-up dummies as instruments for expected inflation.

A second reason for concern about the specification is that inclusion of observations for 1975(3)–1976(4) gives rise to unsatisfactory results in terms of both overall fit and the economic interpretation of the coefficients. This structural break in the functional realtionship though explicable *ex post* in terms of changing aspiration levels or adjustment speeds, may signify deeper problems with the underlying empirical specification.

The next contribution we consider is by Minford and Brech (1981) who estimate wage equations for a number of different countries and give explicit attention to the impact of incomes policies in the United Kingdom. Their analysis is noteworthy for a number of reasons. First the theoretical derivation of their wage equation is based on the hypothesis of a labour market which is assumed to comprise two sectors, a union and non-union sector. In the union sector the desired nominal wage chosen is obtained by the union leadership maximising the discounted value of its potential members' utility, which has real wages and employment as arguments, subject to the constraint of the demand function for labour. The formal mathematics of their analysis need not concern us here (see Minford, 1980 for a fuller exposition). The result is that the rate of change of wages in the union sector depends on the expected rate of inflation and measures of uncertainty of price and quantities, as well as the expected level of the competitive sector real wages and a lagged term reflecting costs of adjustment.

The competitive sector of the Minford and Brech model is assumed to be continuously cleared by non-contract real wages. Consequently, the competitive real wage is determined by the interaction of demand and supply factors (such as the real social security benefit rates, tax rates, and labour force trends) and also by the determinants of the unionised real wage since employment in the union sector feeds back on the competitive sector by withdrawing labour from it. The aggregate nominal wages are a weighted average of wage increases in the union and non-union sector. For convenience Minford and Brech assume that aggregate wage rate statistics record only unionised rates and employ this as their dependent variable. Secondly, Minford and Brech assume that expectations are formed rationally.

The basic wage equation they estimate in the absence of incomes policies is given by

$$w = \alpha_0 + \alpha_1 p^e + \alpha_2 B_{-1} + \alpha_3 T X_{-1} + \alpha_4 t + \alpha_5 Q + \alpha_6 VARP_{-1}$$
$$+ \alpha_7 VARE_{-1} + \alpha_8 \log(R_{-1}) + \alpha_9 PRES_{-1} \tag{2.37}$$

where w is the rate of change of the national wage rate index expressed at an annual rate, p^e is the expected change in retail prices over the coming year, B the ratio of unemployment benefits to earnings, TX the marginal tax rate, Q a measure of expected demand pressure, $VARP$ the variance of unanticipated inflation, $VARE$ the variance of unanticipated employment, R real wages, and $PRES$ unanticipated inflation.

Their data are quarterly for 1960(1) to 1975(4) and they use Tarling and Wilkinson's (1977) incomes policy periods. The constraint that $\alpha_1 = 1$ is imposed in estimation and then subsequently tested using a standard F − test. They estimate (2.37) for those periods there is no incomes policy and they report empirical results which support their hypothesis. In particular the coefficients on the lagged real wage and expected pressure of demand variables are significantly different from zero with the correct *a priori* signs. No significant effects are found for the tax and benefit variables and so they are omitted in the UK analysis.

Minford and Brech consider a number of ways by which incomes policies could modify their wage equations. They use income policy dummies to allow for effects before ($D1$), and after ($D4$) their implementation and also two types of policy: a freeze ($D2$) and other policies ($D3$). They find evidence of a slight positive effect, especially in the periods before and after the policies. Minford and Brech suggest that whilst it is not the intention of these policies to have this positive effect, politicisation of the wage process could lead to some groups getting more (and others less) than the economic conditions alone would dictate.

However there are reasons for questioning Minford and Brech's results. The major problem concerns their modelling of expected inflation by using the predicted value taken from a regression of actual inflation on either domestic or world money supply. In other words their method of obtaining expected inflation is the instrumental–variables procedure of McCallum (1975, 1976) but they make an *ad hoc* adjustment to the predicted series by keeping expected inflation fixed at a value of 10 per cent through the period 1973(4) to 1975(2) even though the actual values in the instruments equation fall from 9.4 per cent in 1973(4) to 0 in 1975(2). The statistical properties of such a procedure are somewhat unclear.

Moreover Minford and Brech report the following relationship between unanticipated inflation and the four incomes policies dummies which they utilise.

$$p - p^e = 0.034 \ - \ 0.034D1 \ - \ 0.0327D2 \ - \ 0.0436D3$$
$$\quad\ (2.35) \quad\quad (-2.58) \quad\quad\ (-2.08) \quad\quad\ (-2.79) \quad\quad (2.38)$$
$$-0.0577D4$$
$$\quad (4.68)$$

$\bar{R}^2 = 0.3052 \ DW = 0.4028$

where t values are in parentheses.

The low Durbin–Watson statistic is explained by the use of overlapping data since p is the four quarter rate of change (see Holden, Peel and Thompson, 1985). Minford and Brech comment on this empirical result and simply state that it appears that incomes policies caused an unanticipated rise in inflation especially before and after the policies. However, unless the incomes policies periods are all regarded as unanticipated, which is *a priori* implausible, the reported empirical results imply serious mis-specification. Under the rational expectations hypothesis all systematic policies should have their influence on expected inflation, not on the difference between actual and expected inflation. The implicit mis-specification of the expected inflation term suggests that the role of incomes policies in the wage equation *per se* will not be properly estimated. It follows therefore that the conclusions of Minford and Brech that incomes policies have no virtuous effects on nominal wages must be interpreted with extreme caution. Further empirical work using their specification but making appropriate allowance for incomes policies on expected inflation may well result in different conclusions.

The final contribution on wage determinants and incomes policy which we consider is by Sumner and Ward (1983). This study uses quarterly UK data for the period 1956(2)–1980(4) and updates the earlier study by Parkin, Sumner and Ward (1976). The model adopted by Sumner and Ward is interesting in that it provides an explicit role for both the expectations of employees and employers in the wage determination process. The range of expectational variables arises from the difference between the product wage paid by employers and the real wage received by employees. The product wage includes employers' social security contributions paid at a rate T_e on the nominal wage W, and is deflated by the wholesale price which firms receive for their output P_e. Employees' income tax and social security contributions are paid at the effective rate, T_c, and their real wage is defined in terms of the retail price index, P_c. The demand and supply of labour are written as log-linear functions of the product wage and real wage respectively.

Consequently

$$D = D\left(\frac{W(1+T_e)}{P_e}\right)^{-\alpha}$$

$$S = S\left(\frac{W(1-T_c)}{P_c}\right)^{\beta}$$

Proportionate excess demand is represented as

$$X = (D-S)/S = \log D - \log S$$

(using the approximation $\log(1+X) \simeq X$)

The expected change in excess demand, $E(\Delta X)$ over the wage contract period is given by

$$E(\Delta X) = -\alpha(w + t^e - p_e^e) - \beta(w + r^e - p_c^e) \tag{2.39}$$

where t^e is the anticipated change in employers' social security contributions and $r^e = \log(1 - T_c^e)/(1 - T_c)$ is the anticipated rate of change of the retention ratio. The next behavioural hypothesis is that nominal wages are set so as to eliminate all or part of realised excess demand during some previous period. (See Parkin, Sumner and Ward, 1976.) This hypothesis is written as

$$\Delta X^e = -\theta X \tag{2.40}$$

where θ is a constant.

Rearrangement of (2.39) and (2.40) gives the basic equation to be estimated which is

$$w = \frac{\theta}{\alpha + \beta} X + \frac{\alpha}{\alpha + \beta} p_c^e + \frac{\beta}{\alpha + \beta} p_e^e - \frac{\alpha}{\alpha + \beta} t^e - \frac{\beta}{\alpha + \beta} r^e \tag{2.41}$$

We notice from (2.41) that the coefficients on the anticipated inflation terms sum to unity and to minus unity on the anticipated tax and retention ratio variables. In their empirical tests Sumner and Ward proxy excess demand by a moving average of past values of the unemployment rate.

The data on firms' price expectations are directly observed survey data obtained from the CBI. Employees' expectations of inflation in the original Parkin, Sumner and Ward study are Gallup data on consumer price expectations. However, for the extended period used by Sumner and Ward they are proxied by the actual rate of change of retail prices lagged one quarter. This procedure, according to Sumner and Ward, minimises simultaneity problems. Unfortunately mis-specification is not a suitable method of dealing with these problems. Consequently a more appropriate interpretation of their procedure is that price expectations of employees are modelled by a simple adaptive expectations scheme. The variable t^e is proxied by a one quarter lag on actual changes and r^e by the actual changes. Sumner and Ward estimate variants of (2.41) for a number of periods. These led to amendments being made to the equation. First, because r^e is always insignificant, with an incorrect sign up to 1970, zero values are imposed until the end of 1970. The new variable is denoted r^*.

Secondly, a dummy variable is introduced for 1978(2). At this time the annualised rate of wage inflation jumped from an average of 6.3 per cent in the preceding four quarters to 36.8 per cent then fell to an average of 11.5 per cent in the following four quarters. They suggest this may be the result of 'catch-up' effects following Phase 2 of the Social Contract. In the absence of the dummy variable many of the variables in the wage equation are insignificant. Thirdly, Sumner and Ward found that the only way to make employees' expectations enter as a significant variable for the whole period is to impose a value of zero in the period up to the end of 1969 and the previous quarter's actual inflation rate in the subsequent periods. This variable is denoted by p_c^*.

Sumner and Ward report the following result for the period 1958(3)–1980(4)

$$w = 5.11 - 1.10U + 0.76p_c^e + 0.18p_c^* - 0.20t^e - 0.58r^*$$
$$\quad\quad (2.15) \quad (5.54) \quad (1.82) \quad (1.62) \quad (3.95)$$
$$+ 29.01D \quad\quad \bar{R}^2 = 0.75 \; DW = 1.75 \quad\quad\quad (2.42)$$
$$(7.71)$$

w is the quarterly rate of change of weekly wage rates and D is the dummy variable for 1978(2). The equation was estimated with an allowance for first order serial correlation of the residuals. However, Sumner and Ward are unhappy about the interpretation of the serial correlation in (2.42) and consequently look for an economic rationale for its presence. They experiment with the addition of a number of incomes policy dummies for the periods 1966(3)–1967(2), 1972(4)–1973(1), 1975(3)–1976(2), 1976(3)–1977(2), 1977(3)–1978(2) and 1978(3)–1979(1). No allowance is made for catch-up effects. The only significant incomes policy dummy they identify is for 1976(3)–1977(2). This period is Phase 2 of the Social Contract. Their best result is the following estimated equation where no allowance has been made for autocorrelation:

$$w = 4.86 \; - 1.02U + 0.73p_c^e + 0.30p^* - 0.24t^e \quad\quad\quad (2.43)$$
$$\quad (5.44) \quad (2.90) \quad (7.03) \quad (3.57) \quad (2.09)$$
$$- 0.55r^* + 28.03D - 10.13I$$
$$\quad (3.64) \quad\quad (7.21) \quad\quad (4.91)$$
$$\bar{R}^2 = 0.77 \quad\quad\quad DW = 1.72$$

where I is the incomes policy dummy for 1976(3)–1977(2). Sumner and Ward point out that the significance of the incomes policy dummy (I) may be attributed to an expectational jolt caused by the fiscal and monetary package that was not recorded in p^*.

Whilst the empirical results reported by Sumner and Ward appear impressive there are a number of questions concerning their analysis. First, the *ad hoc* amendments to the expectational variables appear to be dictated more by properties of the data than by theoretical considerations. Secondly, their estimated equations are apparently not consistent with their theoretical model which implies equal and opposite coefficients on p_c^e and t^e, and p^* and r^*. These restrictions are not supported by the data. This could of course be due to the assumed expectation mechanisms being incorrect. Further work might explicitly allow for and test the validity of these constraints. Thirdly, the important behavioural assumption (2.40) is arbitrary and appears to have no theoretical rationale. Why should negotiators not set wages so that the expected excess demand is zero rather than some arbitrary level?

Fourthly, the information assumptions underlying the demand and supply of labour are questionable in quarterly data. Agents are assumed to have knowledge of the current price levels relevant to their decisions. If this assumption is relaxed the definition of the expectations variables will be changed. In particular p_c^e will be defined as

$$E_{-1} \ln P_c - E_{-2} \ln P_{c-1} \text{ and not } E_{-1} \ln P_c - \ln P_{c-1}$$

where E_{-1} is the expectations operator based on the information set dated $t-1$. Fifthly, it seems unnecessary, and a potential source of misspecification, to proxy excess demand by a weighted average of the current and lagged unemployment rate, when the economic determinants of the demand and supply have been specified. These should be entered directly into (2.41). Finally, the specification of the demand and supply of labour appears to be too simplistic. For example, the demand for labour function omits variables such as the real price of capital services. Similarly the supply of labour function omits interest rate and benefits variables. If such variables are important determinants of the demand and supply of labour then the wage equation will be misspecified. This could explain the serially correlated disturbance terms obtained in some of the results. For these reasons the empirical results of Sumner and Ward should be interpreted with caution.

From our review of these four studies it would be premature to come to any firm conclusion as to the impact of incomes policies on wage determination. The research considered suffers from a number of specification errors which cast doubt on any conclusions obtained by the authors. A major weakness of these studies is in the modelling of price expectations. In future empirical work the impact of incomes policies on price expectations should be recognised. Also the empirical finding of money illusion might be regarded as a sign of mis-specification.

We have reviewed the impact of incomes policies on wages and so we now turn to the impact of incomes policies on prices. We begin by considering the major theoretical underpinnings for almost all of the behavioural equations which are estimated.

2.8 THE PRICE EQUATION

As with the wage equation we consider first the theoretical specification of the price equation and then examine some empirical studies of the impact of incomes policies on prices. The majority of models of price determination are of the form

$$p = \alpha_1 + \alpha_2 w_{-r} + \alpha_3 m_{-s} + \alpha_4 q_{-t} \tag{2.44}$$

where α_1 to α_4 are constants
  m is the rate of change of import prices
  q is the rate of change of productivity
  w is the rate of change of unit labour costs
  $-r, -s, -t$ are lags.

The usual rationale for this specification is based on a cost–plus approach to price determination. Lipsey and Parkin (1970) explicitly derive such an equation. They write down the identity that relates the market value of final output to the value of measured costs, the value of unmeasured costs and residual profits, all expressed as amounts per unit of output (in the absence of taxes). Consequently

$$P = WL + MT + CD + \Pi \tag{2.45}$$

where P = market price of final output
  W = price per unit of labour
  L = quantity of labour used per unit of output
  M = price per unit of imported materials
  T = quantity of imports per unit of output
  C = price per unit of other inputs (called unmeasured inputs)
  D = quantity of unmeasured inputs per unit of output
  Π = profit per unit of output.

In order to give their model some behavioural content Lipsey and Parkin make the following assumptions:
1. the quantity of imports per unit of output (T) is constant
2. unmeasured costs (CD) are a constant fraction (μ) of measured costs $(WL + MT)$

3. firms aim for a constant proportional mark up β and hence aim for Π $= \beta P$ and

4. firms' expectations of W, L and M, (W^*, L^*, and M^* respectively) are generated by the scheme $W^* = W_{-r}$, $M^* = M_{-s}$, and $L^* = L_{-t}$.

Substituting the above assumptions into (2.45) yields

$$P = \frac{(1+\mu)}{1-\beta} (W_{-r}L_{-t} + M_{-s}T) \tag{2.46}$$

Differentiating with respect to time and dividing by P,

$$p = K \left(\frac{W_{-r}L_{-t}}{P}\right) w_{-r} + K \left(\frac{M_{-s}T}{P}\right) m_{-s} - K \left(\frac{W_{-r}L_{-t}}{P}\right) q_{-t} \tag{2.47}$$

where $K = (1+\mu)/1 - \beta$.

This is the same form as (2.44) and Lipsey and Parkin write it as

$$p = \beta_0 w_{-r} + \beta_1 m_{-s} + \beta_2 q_{-t} \tag{2.48}$$

They point out that the coefficient on productivity change (β_2) should be equal but opposite in sign to that on wage change (β_0). Though their analysis appears attractive as a method of rationalising a mark-up price equation in rates of change form there are problems. In order to estimate (2.48) using ordinary least squares it is necessary to assume that β_0, β_1 and β_2 are constants. However, if this is the case, their derivatives with respect to time must be zero.

For example the time derivative of β_1 is

$$\frac{\partial \beta_1}{\partial t} = \frac{1}{P^2} \left\{ PKT\frac{\partial M_{-s}}{\partial t} - KMT\frac{\partial P}{\partial t} \right\} = \frac{KMT}{P}(m-p) \tag{2.49}$$

For this to be zero, m and p must be equal which conflicts with (2.48).

In fact the appropriate way to test the mark-up hypothesis appears to be to estimate a price level equation. (Wallis (1971) also argues for the estimation of price level equations though for rather different reasons). We note however that (2.45) is an identity and behavioural assumptions are needed to give it explanatory power. We now turn to the literature on the impact of incomes policies on prices.

The first study we consider is by Lipsey and Parkin (1970) who estimate equations of the form (2.44) and who use the policy-on/policy-off methodology already discussed in relation to the wage equation. They report results which suggest that the price equation changes substantially during the periods of incomes policy. In fact, unlike periods when the policy is off, when incomes policies are in operation only the productivity change variable is significant. However, as with their wage equations, authors such as Wallis (1971) and Godfrey (1971) point out that their results are quite different when allowance is made for serial correlation and the endogeneity of variables. Also there are the theoretical problems (mentioned above) which imply that (2.44) is mis-specified. This point applies to a large number of other papers based on the mark-up hypothesis (see Smith, 1972; Burrows and Hitiris, 1972, for the UK; and Gordon, 1970; and Eckstein and Brinner, 1972, for the US). Further empirical research on the impact of incomes policies in behavioural price equations is necessary before the conclusions of Lipsey and Parkin (1970) and Parkin, Sumner and Jones (1972) that the existing evidence indicates that incomes policies have no identifiable effect on the behavioural price equation can be accepted.

A study which uses intervention analysis to examine the impact of the Nixon administration Phase I (Sept., Oct., Nov., 1971) and Phase II (Dec. 1971–Dec. 1972) controls on consumer prices in the US is that by Box and Tiao (1975). They examine monthly data over the period July 1953 to December 1972 giving 234 observations. The ARIMA process generating consumer prices was identified prior to the implementation of controls and then intervention analysis is used to examine the impact of the two periods of controls. The prices variable p_t is the monthly rate of change of the Consumer Price Index and the estimated models are

$$p_t - p_{t-1} = e_t - 0.84\,e_{t-1}$$
$$(21.0)$$

before the introduction of controls, where e_t is a random error term, and the t-value is in parentheses, and

$$p_t = -0.0022\,D_1 - 0.0008D_2 + (e_t - 0.85e_{t-1})/(1-L)$$
$$(2.2) \qquad\qquad (0.9) \qquad\qquad (17.0)$$

when price controls are introduced. Here D_1 and D_2 are the dummy variables for Phase I and Phase II, and L is the lag operator. The negative coefficients on both D_1 and D_2 are as expected but only the Phase I controls have a significant effect. Of course as with the wage equation, the 'reduced form' method does not explain the mechanism by which controls influence consumer prices (e.g. through wages or profit margins, etc.).

Feige and Pearce (1976) also use intervention analysis to examine the impact of the Nixon administration's Phase I and Phase II controls on the consumer price index, and the wholesale price index. They use monthly data over the period 1953(2) and 1971(8). Unlike Box and Tiao they find that none of the dummy variables have coefficients which are significantly different from zero. This lack of conformity of results is interesting and may be due to the slightly different data periods, given that both sets of results appear to identify the same ARIMA process for consumer prices in the absence of controls. The sensitivity of these results to a few observations of course creates difficulties in their interpretation.

The feeling which emerges from this review of the more influential empirical studies of the impact of incomes policies on either wage or price determination is that much of the work is flawed and the final results are not convincing. In addition to the points already raised, a further matter concerns the way in which incomes policies are modelled. Previous work has endeavoured to model the impact when incomes policies are in operation or in the period immediately following their termination. However, the effects of the anticipation of a future incomes policy have been ignored. For example, if agents expect a wage freeze backed by sanctions to be imposed in six months time this will have implications for the length of contracts and size of settlements in current negotiations. This anticipations effect has been essentially neglected in previous work. Implicitly, researchers have assumed that periods of incomes policies are unexpected. One interesting possibility for future work is to introduce into behavioural equations not only dummy variables representing the effects of incomes policies but also some empirical measure of the probabilities of implementation of different forms of policies for different future time periods. The recent empirical work of Desai, Keil and Wadhwani (1984) and others discussed in section 2.10 below suggests how this might be done.

Several authors, including Ashenfelter and Pencavel (1975) and Taylor (1980) have considered the implications of incomes policies on wage determination in a framework which gives explicit attention to contract length or the frequency of settlement. In Canada, Christofides (1985) found that a significant shortening of contracts occurred when incomes policies were in operation. Unfortunately this work did not allow for any anticipations effects.

Finally, as well as modelling the direct and indirect effects of incomes policies, future work must also allow for effects through price expectations, as shown in (2.27). Given all these points we suggest that the sentiments expressed by Oi (1976) after his review of earlier work is still valid. He wrote (p. 47) 'the empirical evidence assembled by either the defenders or opponents of wage–price controls is unlikely to have a significant impact in varying the numbers in the two camps'.

Given the methodological difficulties in interpreting the aggregate empirical evidence of the impact of incomes policies on wages and prices we now turn to further consideration of the *a priori* case for these policies.

2.9 MICROECONOMIC IMPLICATIONS

While the effects of incomes policies on aggregate wages and prices are important, their impact on resource allocation also require examination. In particular, the evasion of controls by firms will be considered as will the varying impacts on different sectors of the economy. Our discussion is in terms of price controls but similar arguments apply to wage controls.

As a start to the analysis we begin by considering the possible impact of controls on an individual firm or market. Suppose for simplicity that the authorities have set a price ceiling. For this to influence the behaviour of the firm, violation of the control should have an implicit cost or shadow price. Whether the firm complies with the control will depend on the penalties (possibly fines or loss of goodwill of customers) imposed on the firm for violating the control and also the firm's assessment of the probability of detection.

This can be demonstrated by using the model developed by Pencavel (1981). Define a firm's profit function by

$$\Pi = \Pi(P, R) \tag{2.50}$$

where P is the price of the firm's output

R is the vector of prices paid for the firm's inputs.

Let P_c be the controlled price imposed by the authorities where $P_c < P$. Let D be the fine imposed on the firm for not complying with the policy and θ the firm's assessment of the probability of violation of the control being detected by the authorities. With these assumptions the expected profits of the firm can be written as

$$E(\Pi) = (1 - \theta)\Pi(P, R) + \theta\Pi(P_c, R) - \theta D \tag{2.51}$$

The employer will not comply with the control if

$$E(\Pi) > \Pi(P_c, R) \tag{2.52}$$

Combining (2.52) with (2.51) we obtain the following condition for non-compliance

$$[\Pi(P, R) - \Pi(P_c, R)] > \frac{\theta}{1-\theta}D \qquad (2.53)$$

Equation (2.53) illustrates that an employer is, *ceteris paribus*, more likely to comply with the price control, the greater the penalty D, the greater the probability of detection (θ) and the smaller the gap between profits without regulation, and profits with controls.

When compliance occurs the initial effects will depend upon the structure of the particular markets. Consider initially a competitive market. In Figure 2.2 we depict the demand and supply curves for a commodity which yields, in the absence of price controls, an equilibrium price and quantity of P_0 and Q_0. If we introduce a price ceiling P_1 the new price and quantity combination is P_1 and Q_1, assuming that firms commit no resources to evasion of the policy. Consequently both price and output are lower than in the non-regulated case. Furthermore, at the new price demand is greater than supply and consequently there are shortages. The amount of unsatisfied demand increases with (a) the

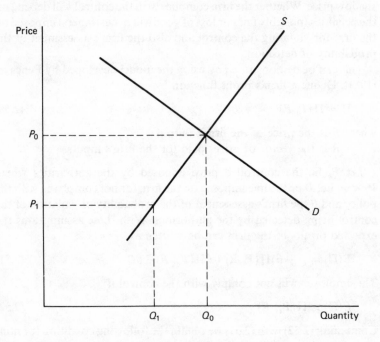

Figure 2.2

degree to which prices diverge from their equilibrium values and (b) the sum of the absolute values of the slopes of the demand and supply curves. This is illustrated mathematically by Pencavel (1981). If firms commit resources to evasion then this shifts the supply curve to the left and gives rise to the situation depicted in Figure 2.3. The non-compliance price will be greater than P_1 and less than or equal to the new equilibrium price P_3. We notice that for any non-compliance price output is less than in the non-regulated case (Q_0) and that for any price less than P_3 there are shortages.

The implications of price controls for a monopolist are somewhat different from those for the competitive market and are discussed by Darby (1976). We consider first the case where the monopolist does not devote any resources to avoidance and consequently complies with the controls. Assuming profit maximisation, in Figure 2.4 market equilibrium is determined by the intersection of the marginal cost and marginal revenue curves. The price P_0 is the 'height' of the demand curve at the quantity Q_0. When price controls are complied with the marginal revenue curve is a horizontal line at the controlled price P_1 up to its intersection with the demand curve and from that quantity up corresponds to the original marginal revenue curve. (The firm's effective

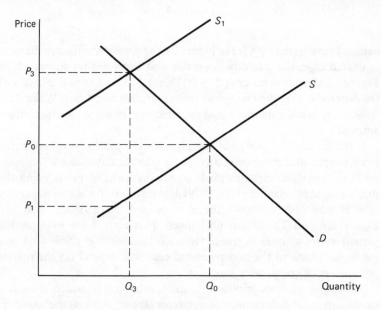

Figure 2.3

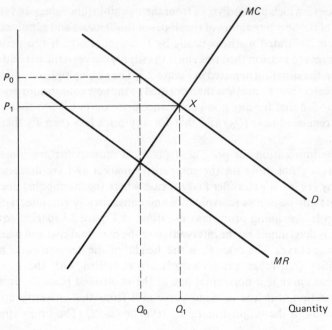

Figure 2.4

demand curve is the $P_1 XD$.) In Figure 2.4 the price is less than in the non-regulated case, the quantity is greater and there are no shortages. In Figure 2.5 shortages occur ($Q_1^d > Q_1^s$) since P_1 is less than the height of the demand curve when it intersects the marginal cost curve. When P_1 is sufficiently low the quantity sold may decrease beneath the equilibrium amount.

If the monopolist does not comply with the price controls then the price/output configuration relative to the non-regulated case will depend on the precise assumptions made about the form of penalty and the firm's attitude to risk (see Hey, 1979). For instance, if it is a fixed penalty then it may only influence the average cost curve of the firm and Figures 2.4 and 2.5 remain unchanged. However, if for example the penalty varies with the degree of violation then whether prices are lower (or higher) than in the non-regulated case will depend on the precise parameters of the penalty function.

The above analysis implies that in an economy in which there is a significant monopoly element in goods (or labour) markets the introduction of price (or wage) controls could move the economy closer to the

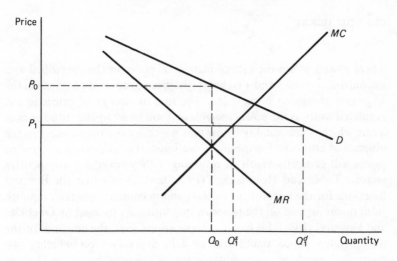

Figure 2.5

competitive one. However, as pointed out by a number of authors (Pencavel, 1981) this argument for an incomes policy or price controls must be evaluated relative to other measures which could reduce the resource misallocation impact of monopolies such as antitrust legislation, the reform of trade unions, tax-based income policies or final offer arbitration (see Chapters 3 and 4). Furthermore, the monopoly argument for controls implies that in the face of continuing inflationary pressure, due (say) to a given monetary policy, effective controls (which from (2.53) implies penalties increasing at least at the rate of inflation in the sector) will ultimately lead to shortages as monopoly elements are eliminated. Although the analysis above demonstrates that price controls may have an impact on a particular sector there are a number of factors which must be allowed for in considering their potential impact on the aggregate economy. The first point is that generally, either by design or by incentive, price controls will not *directly* affect all sectors in the economy. In other words some sectors will be exempt or not comply with the controls. For example, in the UK it is generally true that the low paid have been excluded from incomes policies and the prices of seasonal foods from price controls.

Following Oi (1976) it is useful to think of the economy as constituting a regulated and unregulated sector. Given this assumption, the aggregate rate of change in the measured price index can be written as a weighted average of the rates of change of controlled and uncontrolled prices. We can write this as

$$p = \lambda p^c + (1 - \lambda)p^u$$

where p^c and p^u are the rate of change of prices in the controlled and uncontrolled sectors and λ is the weight given to controlled goods in the aggregate measured price index. The rate of change of prices in the regulated sector is the policy variable and will be set by the authorities at a rate which is presumably below that which is expected to occur in the absence of controls. Furthermore we know that effectively controlled prices will generally result in rationing if they cover any competitive sectors. Tobin and Houthakker (1951) have shown that the demand functions for the uncontrolled goods and in consequence their equilibrium prices depend on the rationed quantities. As stressed by Oi (1976) and Pencavel (1981) this has two implications. First the demand for the uncontrolled goods could rise or fall, depending on whether the controlled goods are substitutable for or complementary to the uncontrolled goods. This effect could lead to sectors which were initially uninfluenced by the controls becoming subject to their influence. The relative price shift induced by the incomes policy could in principle leave the aggregate measured price (or wage) index uninfluenced by price controls or even in exceptional cases lead to greater increases than in their absence.

Secondly, the measured price index is an inappropriate method of measuring inflation if we are concerned about the impact of inflation on the welfare of consumers (see Oi, 1976). The appropriate measure of inflation should be a weighted average of prices in the uncontrolled sector and the shadow prices (or support prices) of the goods in the controlled sector. It follows that empirical studies which use aggregate measured prices may produce a potentially biased measure of the impact of controls on consumer welfare to the extent that the controlled and shadow prices differ.

So far the analysis of the impacts of controls on prices has been conducted as if a good has unidimensional characteristics. Alternatively following Lancaster (1971) we can think of any good as a bundle of characteristics which are bought at a certain price. If the authorities control, for example, the price of a car, the manufacturer can in principle respond by changing the quality of the product. This is known as a change in the 'hedonic' price. Such action is of course not costless since it may involve negotiation time or changes in the production process. The authorities may attempt to introduce penalties for such changes in the hedonic price but if the perceived probabilities of detection are low, non-compliance by firms may be high.

However, if such changes in the physical characteristics of the product do not occur it implies that the price controls have led to the suppression of a low-cost signalling method by which resources can be allocated in response to shifts in demand or supply. Thus price controls may cause a real deadweight loss in the economy due to the misallocation of resources involved in non-price rationing.

Finally, we should note that an appropriate measure of the welfare costs of price controls should make explicit allowance for the resources which are used by the authorities in implementing the policy.

It is clear from the above discussion that price (and also wage) controls which are backed by either formal penalties (such as fines) or informal penalties (such as loss of goodwill of customers) and where the firm perceives a finite probability of detection will have an impact on economic activity. In particular, relative measured prices in the economy will change given the degree of effective control in each sector of the economy. Prices in the controlled sector are likely to fall relative to prices in the uncontrolled sector. Furthermore, it is likely that the hedonic price of goods in the controlled sector will rise relative to goods in the uncontrolled sector.

2.10 THE POLITICAL RATIONALE

The potential microeconomic effects of price controls have led Cox (1980) to suggest a rationale for the implementation of controls by the authorities. He considers the implications of assuming that the authorities wish to maximise political support by the use of price controls. However, this support is maximised subject to the constraints that (a) effective price controls require expenditures in the form of enforcement costs and (b) that whilst a deceleration in the rate of measured inflation increases political support, the non-price rationing and misallocation of resources effects due to controls decrease political popularity. The authorities are assumed to trade off the effects of a price ceiling on aggregate measured inflation against the effects of a price ceiling on excess demand for each industry. Because enforcement is more costly in some industries than others, and assuming the authorities only have finite resources to devote to enforcement of controls, it follows that more enforcement in one industry implies less enforcement in others. The crux of the Cox hypothesis is that

> the price controllers weigh the political returns from a price ceiling against the enforcement cost for each industry, and they take account of the foregone political support from enforcing price controls in one industry rather than elsewhere. The result is that some industries will have effective price ceilings and others will not. Where the controls are effective, the extent to which prices are held below the equilibrium level will differ between industries. (Cox, 1980, p. 889)

Cox next considers in more detail the relationship between political support and price controls. One obvious way in which controls may elicit support is through their impact on the measured price index. However this argument depends on the electorate suffering from the illusion that controls are *ceteris paribus* an effective method of curing inflation. If inflation is a monetary phenomenon then price controls will not of course reduce the forces which would produce upward movements in the aggregate price index in the absence of controls. These pressures will ultimately cause a misallocation of resources (the possible initial favourable effects on the monopoly sector eroding over time) which could cause a net decrease in political support. Cox suggests that the typically short period of controls is consistent with the hypothesis of short-run illusion. However, he points out that the argument that controls lead to political support does not depend solely on the illusion hypothesis. This is because controls will redistribute income. The beneficiaries will be those buyers who can acquire goods under the non-price rationing schemes which result from the controls and these buyers will provide political support for the government. The political-support rationale for controls can thus be explained either by the illusion hypothesis or by the income redistribution approach.

Using US data for a cross-section of industries for the period August 1971 to April 1974, Cox provides some subtle empirical analysis which is consistent with his hypothesis. In particular his empirical work suggests that when controls are in effect, prices are held down more where political benefits are high, political costs are low and enforcement costs are low.

As Cox points out, an interesting extension of his analysis is to examine whether there are industries which benefit because input prices are more stringently controlled relative to product prices, and the relationship of such industries to the political process (see also Nuti, 1969).

Some empirical support for the hypothesis that political support is influenced by incomes policies is provided by Desai, Keil and Wadhwani (1984). Using quarterly UK data they find that the lead of the government over the main opposition, as measured by opinion-poll data is, *ceteris paribus*, positively associated with incomes policies lagged one period but negatively related to incomes policies lagged five periods. However the sum of the coefficients on the incomes policy dummies is negative. Pencavel (1981) also reports that the Gallup Poll of US public at large indicates that in only one survey in the 30 years between 1946 and 1979 did the majority of respondents express an unfavourable view on the merits of wage–price controls.

It would thus appear that incomes policies may, *ceteris paribus*, result in an increase in political support for the authorities at least in the short run. Three empirical studies by Desai, Keil and Wadhwani (1984) and Holden and Peel (1985) using UK data and Pencavel (1981) using US data have endeavoured to explain the decision by the authorities to implement an incomes policy. Their work follows a suggestion originally made by Wallis (1971) who wrote 'the decision to impose an incomes policy is not independent of the values of the model, and although treated as exogenous in the Lipsey–Parkin study the policy itself must surely also become a jointly dependent endogenous variable' (Wallis, 1971, p. 309). Desai, Keil and Wadhwani use logit analysis (see e.g. McFadden, 1974) to analyse the impact of a variety of variables on the probability of implementation of an incomes policy. The 'political variables' used are the parliamentary majority of the government over all the other parties (MAJ), a dummy variable which indicates the time to the next general election (NG), the balance of the Gallup sample that approve of incomes policy (POP), and the lead of the government over the main opposition party relative to a measure of the desired lead (LEAD). The economic variables used are the lagged one quarter rate of change of the gross domestic product deflator (P_{t-1}), the lagged one quarter rate of change of output per man (pr_{t-1}), the lagged one quarter change in the spot dollar exchange rate (EX_{t-1}) the lagged one quarter rate of change of average hourly earnings in manufacturing (e_{t-1}), the lagged four quarters logarithm of real hourly earnings in manufacturing ($e - p)_{t-4}$ incomes policy lagged one period (IPD_{t-1}) and the stock of official reserves (OR_{t-1}).

One empirical result obtained by Desai, Keil and Wadhwani is (with $-$ Log odds of having incomes policy ON (IPD) as the dependent variable)

$$IPD = -3.63NG - 0.062MAJ - 0.89LEAD + 1.45POP$$
$$\quad (1.79) \qquad (1.49) \qquad\quad (1.68) \qquad\quad (1.83) \qquad\qquad (2.54)$$

$$\qquad + 59.86P_{t-1} - 53.10pr_{t-1} - 20.4EX_{t-1} + 20.28e_{t-1}$$
$$\qquad\quad (1.02) \qquad\quad (1.49) \qquad\quad (1.16) \qquad\quad (0.35)$$

$$\qquad + 19.57(e-p)_{t-4} + 8.66IPD_{t-1} \quad (t \text{ values in parentheses})$$
$$\qquad\quad (0.79) \qquad\qquad (2.11)$$

Equation (2.54) correctly predicts 97 per cent of incomes policy periods. However, the majority of variables are not significantly different from zero at usual levels of significance. The significant or near significant variables are NG with a negative coefficient, $LEAD$ with a negative coefficient, IPD with a positive coefficient and POP with a positive coefficient. Consequently this study does not provide any real support for the view that the chosen economic variables effect the probability of implementation of an incomes policy.

Holden and Peel (1985) also use logit analysis to examine some possible determinants of incomes policies in the United Kingdom for 1957–83. They extend the analysis of Desai, Keil and Wadhwani to include the party in power as an additional variable to allow for different economic or political ideologies (see Minford and Peel, 1983). Also, the effects of economic variables differ with the party in power by means of slope dummy variables. Their results, in contrast to those of Desai, Keil and Wadhwani, support the hypothesis that the probability of an incomes policy being implemented depends on both political (popularity, nearness of election, the party in power) and economic (inflation, wage growth, unemployment) factors. *Ceteris paribus*, incomes policies are more probable with a Labour government and the probability rises with increasing unemployment and falls with inflation. With a Conservative government, these effects are reversed. Thus high price and wage inflation and low unemployment make a Conservative government more likely to impose an incomes policy.

Pencavel (1981), using US data, also employs both political and economic variables to explain the probability of implementation of an incomes policy (ID). However, they are different to those employed by the above studies. Pencavel's political variable is the fraction of people expressing approval or no opinion of the President's performance lagged one quarter as measured by the Gallup Opinion Poll (G_{t-1}). The economic variables used are the inverse of the unemployment rate lagged one quarter (U_{t-1}), the annual rate of change of industrial production lagged one quarter (ΔX_{-1}), the annual change in the inverse of the unemployment rate lagged one quarter (ΔU_{t-1}) a weighted average over eight quarters, lagged one quarter, of changes in the annual rate of consumer price inflation $(\Sigma\Delta^2 p_{t-i})$ and a similarly constructed variable for the rate of change of hourly compensation $(\Sigma\Delta^2 W_{t-i})$. The estimation procedure employed by Pencavel is ordinary least squares. One result he reports is

$$ID = 0.347 - 0.559G_{t-1} + 0.049U_{t-1}$$
$$\quad (1.29) \quad (1.80) \qquad (1.53) \qquad\qquad\qquad (2.55)$$

$$\quad - 0.368\Delta U_{t-1} + 3.650\Delta X_{t-1} + 13.173\Sigma\Delta^2 P_{t-i}$$
$$\quad\quad (2.37) \qquad\qquad (5.07) \qquad\qquad (2.48)$$

$$\qquad\qquad\qquad - 14.166\Sigma\Delta^2 W_{t-i}$$
$$\qquad\qquad\qquad\quad (2.12)$$

where t-values are in parentheses.

Unfortunately the ordinary least squares method of estimation is not appropriate when the dependent variable is of the one-zero form, since it leads to biased estimates of the standard errors of the coefficients and consequently significance tests on the estimated coefficients are not valid.

Whilst the signs of the coefficients in equation (2.55) are *a priori* plausible, clearly, alternative estimation procedures are required before the significance of the economic variables can be evaluated.

Although these results are provisional, there is enough evidence to show that periods of incomes policies can be predicted. This strengthens our earlier observations about the failure of previous empirical work to discriminate between the effects of incomes policies when in operation and the impact due to their anticipation. Future empirical work should also consider two further points. First, the logit estimation method requires periods to be classified as either having incomes policies or not. Thus compulsory freezes are grouped with voluntary zero-norm policies. The use of the multi-logit estimation method would make it possible to have a larger number of categories. Secondly, the choice of economic variables in the analysis implies that the authorities are either naïve or believe in a cost–push model of inflation.

One interesting question is whether there is a rationale for incomes policies in models in which both the authorities and private agents have rational expectations. As we saw above, Cox (1980) has provided a possible political hypothesis for such a policy. We now consider the justification for an incomes policy under the assumption of rational expectations and a monetary model of the inflationary process. Suppose that the authorities are committed to a policy of reducing the rate of inflation. Such a policy requires reductions in the actual and anticipated future rates of monetary expansion. If the fall in the rate of inflation induced by such a policy is more than expected by agents then the rate of unemployment will, *ceteris paribus* rise as *ex post* real wages are higher than anticipated. If the government's policy intentions are credible then announced changes in future monetary conditions would influence expectations and monetary contraction has little impact on real activity in a variety of models of the economy (see Minford and Peel, 1983). However, if the government's announcements are not credible then such a contractionary policy will cause real output to fall and the unemployment rate to rise. This credibility problem provides one reason for incomes policies even assuming rational expectations in a monetary model.

Suppose for instance that inflation is currently 15 per cent and the authorities wish to bring it down to, say, 5 per cent over the next year. Furthermore, they believe that an announced change in monetary action consistent with a 5 per cent inflation rate would have little influence on price expectations. One policy action is to implement a temporary incomes policy, limiting wage or price increases to 5 per cent, concurrent with the contractionary monetary policy. This policy can ensure that the real economy is insulated from the unanticipated inflation shock of around 10 per cent which would occur in its absence. The real dislocation caused by such a shock could, in principle, greatly exceed any micro distortions caused by the policy. If the price expectations of agents are formed adaptively then the argument for the use of an incomes policy can also be made.

In future empirical work it will be of interest to test whether such a hypothesis can explain the implementation of incomes policies. In particular the difference between the expected rate of inflation prior to the implementation of the policy and actual inflation which occurs under the policy may be one variable of interest.

2.11 CONCLUSIONS

We now review some of the more important points that have arisen in our discussion of the effects of incomes policies. First, although there has been a great deal of empirical work which has investigated the aggregate impact of incomes policies on either wages or prices there are a number of methodological problems with the specifications used, so that conclusions based on such work may be somewhat dubious. In particular it would appear that future work should pay greater attention to the modelling of expectations variables. The possible effects of the announcement, implementation and future cessation of the policies on expectations are worthy of investigation.

One particular framework in which it might be of interest to investigate such policies is the staggered overlapping contracts models pioneered by Taylor (1980). Two key assumptions underlie Taylor's model – (a) wage contracts are staggered, that is, not all wage decisions in the economy are made at the same times, and (b) when making wage contracts, firms and unions look at the wage rates set by other firms and which will be in effect during their own contract periods. Due to the staggered wage contracts the observed aggregate wage will be a weighted average of wage rates contracted in the current and previous periods.

Incomes policies could influence observed measured wages in at least two ways in this model. First, the announcement, implementation and cessation of an incomes policy may be hypothesised to change the optimal wage contract length. For instance, the announcement of an incomes policy may lead to a shortening of the optimal wage contract so that firms and workers can quickly eliminate 'distortions' caused by the policy on its removal. Secondly, to the extent that wage contracts overlap, the impact of an incomes policy on measured wages when implemented may not be adequately captured by a one-zero dummy. Rather the policy may take some time to 'build up' as contracts negotiated prior to the policy are re-negotiated under the policy. When we considered the analysis that has been undertaken concerning the possible impact of controls at a disaggregated level we found that effective controls would lead to relative price changes between controlled and uncontrolled sectors with the overall result on the measured price or wage indices being unclear. The prediction of the analysis is that controls are likely to lead to excess demand in competitive sectors and consequently non-price rationing and misallocation of real resources. This suggests that future work might consider the impact of incomes policies on aggregate real variables such as output or unemployment.

Cox (1980) shows how the microeconomic effects of incomes policies could provide an additional explanation (to the obvious one of the direct impact on measured wages or prices) as to why incomes policies may be implemented by the authorities. The idea is that the differential incidence of controls can be utilised to maximise political support. Certainly the limited empirical work undertaken using Gallup popularity data suggests that incomes policies are, at least initially, popular with the electorate. The way, if any, by which economic variables influence the probability of implementation of an incomes policy is less clear. The empirical work undertaken so far has, perhaps, not given sufficient attention to the information assumptions which underly the behaviour of the authorities or agents within the economy. These are issues which will undoubtedly be pursued. We conclude this chapter by suggesting that the final decision as to the efficacy of incomes policy, at least in a monetarist framework, should be based on a cost benefit analysis which compares the costs of distortions caused by such a policy when implemented with contractionary monetary policy with those which occur when contractionary monetary policy is implemented alone or in conjunction with other policies. In the next chapter we turn to a relatively new form of wage and price control, the tax-based incomes policy.

3 Tax-Based Incomes Policies

3.1 INTRODUCTION

In this chapter we examine various suggestions for controlling incomes and prices by means of taxes. The original tax-based incomes policy (TIP) proposal of Wallich and Weintraub (1971) imposes tax penalties on firms which make excessive wage increases. It is argued that this stiffens the resistance of firms to inflationary wage claims, resulting in lower settlements and hence lower costs and lower inflation. However, this relies on a cost–push view of inflation. If the rate of inflation is determined by the rate of monetary growth in the long run, then, since the TIP does not affect monetary growth, it cannot have a permanent effect. Instead the TIP can only alter the transition path of inflation as it moves to its steady state value. However, the TIP does alter the nature of the firm's budget constraint and so influences real decisions. An appreciation of this point has resulted in the recent suggestion of using a TIP as a method for reducing the natural rate of unemployment.

The plan of this chapter is as follows. First we outline the original TIP proposal of Wallich and Weintraub. In sections 3.2 and 3.3 we present the analysis of Layard (1982) of the effects of TIP on the level of unemployment. Theoretical criticisms of TIP are discussed in section 3.4 and more general problems in section 3.5. Alternative versions of TIP are reviewed in section 3.6 and the implications of TIP for macroeconomic stability are considered in section 3.7. The conclusions are summarised in section 3.8.

Wallich and Weintraub (1971) viewed the inflation of the late 1960s and early 1970s, as being of the cost–push variety. Wage increases above productivity increases resulted in higher prices which in turn caused workers to demand higher wage increases and so on. Wallich and Weintraub believe that to end this it was necessary to increase the ability of employers to resist inflationary wage settlements. In particular, employers need to know that other employers will also attempt to resist high wage claims.

The solution proposed by Wallich and Weintraub is to introduce an employer penalty TIP in which there is a 'norm' for wage increases and a special surcharge on the profits tax of those firms that agree to settlements above this norm. Thus the tax rate for firm i is

$$t_i = b + m(w_i - n) \quad \text{for } w_i > n$$
$$\quad = b \qquad\qquad\quad \text{for } w_i < n \tag{3.1}$$

where b = base tax rate (per cent)

m = TIP multiplier (a policy parameter)

w_i = average wage increase for firm i (per cent)

n = the norm or target for wage increases (per cent)

In the original formulation t_i is a tax on corporate or business income so that it applies to net profits. A firm making settlements which average at or below the norm will pay tax at the base rate. Those firms that want to agree to settlements above the norm are free to do so but are then penalised by the higher tax rate. The larger m is, the greater the cost. Unions would know that excessive pay rises could only be obtained at a high cost, in terms of profits, to the firm so it is assumed that unions would therefore not press for high wage increases. Management would try to keep settlements low in order to avoid reducing profits. Even if the outcome were to be a high settlement, tax revenue would increase and there would be some deflationary effect in the absence of tax reductions elsewhere.

The use of average wage increases for w allows some variation within the firm and the fact that w can exceed n means that firms which are short of labour can be flexible in their choice of w. Thus some of the distortions of a flat-rate incomes policy can be avoided. Markets are essentially free to operate and meaningful negotiations between the employers and unions can take place.

Wallich and Weintraub present no formal analysis of the impact of their TIP. Because in their view inflation is the cost–push variety the tax is seen simply as a method of strengthening the resolve of firms to resist inflationary wage settlements. Layard (1982) sets out a more formal and detailed analysis of the impact of TIP and we now turn to this.

3.2 LAYARD'S INFLATION TAX PROPOSAL

Layard (1982) suggests an inflation tax for the United Kingdom which is a type of TIP with a penalty imposed on employers who pay excessive wage increases. He presents both macroeconomic and microeconomic models to document the effects of such a tax but does not attempt to reconcile them. In this section we will consider the macroeconomic effects and leave the microeconomic implications to the next section.

The emphasis in Layard's discussion of TIP is on the use of the inflation tax to reduce the level of unemployment. Taking the standard reduced form 'Phillips curve',

$$p = p^e - \gamma(U - U^*) \tag{3.2}$$

where p = the inflation rate
$\quad p^e$ = the expected inflation rate
$\quad U$ = the unemployment rate
$\quad \gamma$ = constant
$\quad U^*$ = non-accelerating inflation rate of unemployment (NAIRU)

then inflation will only be less than expected inflation when U is greater than U^*. If the government endeavours to reduce the rate of inflation then the level of unemployment must rise above the NAIRU if expectations do not respond to the policy changes. However, Layard argues that a TIP can reduce costs directly and can also reduce the expected inflation rate so that p and p^e become equal and unemployment reduces to U^*.

Layard proceeds by considering how U^* might be determined. The wage equation is

$$w = p^e - \gamma(U - U_0) + x^* \tag{3.3}$$

where w = wage inflation, x^* = target real-wage growth rate, γ, U_0 = constants, and the simple price equation

$$p = w - x \tag{3.4}$$

where x = rate of real-wage growth compatible with constant prices.

Thus p is zero when w is x. The value of x will be determined by the growth of productivity and increases in prices of imported raw materials. Substitution of (3.3) into (3.4) gives

$$p = p^e - \gamma\left(U - \left(U_0 + \frac{x^* - x}{\gamma}\right)\right) \tag{3.5}$$

with

$$U^* = U_0 + \frac{x^* - x}{\gamma}$$

by comparison with (3.2). From (3.5), when inflation is constant the long-run unemployment rate will rise if the feasible rate of growth of real wages falls. That is, U^* depends on x and not solely on the structural characteristics of the labour market. Layard quotes evidence that x has fallen by 2.5 percentage points since 1972 in the United Kingdom, which helps to explain the increase in unemployment since then.

The particular proposal for TIP is for the government to announce a norm for hourly earnings growth and any employer who increases average hourly earnings above this norm is taxed on the excess. Notice that this differs from the Wallich and Weintraub proposal to tax profits. In order that the tax will not have a deflationary effect on aggregate demand a rebate scheme would also be introduced with each firm receiving an amount proportional to the firm's total wage bill. The advantages of this are that firms as a group do not suffer compared to workers and the tax will have no net effect on prices. The result is to add the term $- \beta t$ (where t is the tax rate) to (3.3), and hence to (3.5). In the short run even with unchanged price expectations, either the same inflation path can be followed with lower unemployment or the same unemployment path with lower inflation. If the tax also reduces p^e this effect is strengthened. However, in the long run the inflation rate is determined by the rate of growth of money income relative to potential output so that the inflation tax is solely a mechanism for raising the level of employment. We return to this point below.

Layard also discusses some of the details of the tax. In view of the role of the public sector in the United Kingdom (see Chapter 1, section 1.3), he expects local government and the nationalised industries to pay the tax while the central government sector would be exempt but wage increases would equal the norm each year plus any extra payments due as a catch-up if the previous year the private sector increase was above the norm. The tax would be at a high rate, possibly 50 or 100 per cent but would still be worth paying by some firms if they needed extra labour.

The specific wage variable chosen is average hourly earnings paid by the firm. The earnings measure includes all employee compensation as for the PAYE income tax system and so is straightforward. If average earnings per worker were to be used the introduction of a TIP would penalise employers who increased overtime and reward employers who began employing part-time workers at low pay. Measuring hours worked is more of a problem. If only firms with more than 100 workers are involved some record of hours worked is usually needed for pay calculations so this could be used. In the case of salaried employees a nominal figure may be adequate, with explanations required should the nominal figure change. Matthews (1982) suggests that if measuring hours is a problem then limiting the scheme to whole-time workers may be sensible, with average earnings per week as the decision variable.

Layard considers that a TIP along these lines should be introduced on a permanent basis rather than as a temporary policy designed to reduce excessively high inflation at a particular time. This is because, as already noted, in the long run the effect of a TIP is to raise the level of employment. Clearly a temporary policy would have no long-run impact. This aspect of Layard's argument is examined next.

3.3 EFFECTS OF A TIP ON EMPLOYMENT

In their examination of the effects of a TIP, Layard (1982) and Jackman and Layard (1982) proceed on a microeconomic basis as opposed to the macroeconomic discussion in the previous section. The essence of their argument is that the imposition of a tax raises the cost of labour to the firm. Consequently inflationary behaviour is altered with employers resisting more strongly wage claims. Notice that this applies even with the tax being rebated so that the average employer is roughly in the same position as existed before the introduction of the tax. This occurs because the tax is levied on excessive wage awards whereas the rebate is independent of the current wage increase. As a result there would be a redistributive effect with low-wage-increase employers benefiting at the expense of high-wage-increase employers. Similarly, trade unions would know that wage increases above the norm would attract the tax and so reinforce the rise in the firm's labour costs. Consequently the TIP provides an incentive for unions to exercise restraint in wage negotiations.

The argument is developed formally by consideration of three different models of the labour market.

The simplest one assumes that strong unions negotiate with N competitive industries, each with a fraction $1/N$ of the labour force associated with it (see Jackman and Layard, 1982 pp. 232–3). The demand for labour in the ith industry is

$$E_i = a - bW_i \tag{3.6}$$

where E is the employment rate and W is the real wage. The unions maximise the real wage bill (EW) and since

$$EW = aW - bW^2 \tag{3.7}$$

the maximum occurs when

$$W = \frac{a}{2b} \tag{3.8}$$

$$E = \frac{a}{2} \tag{3.9}$$

and so unemployment is

$$1 - E = \frac{a}{2} \tag{3.10}$$

Turning now to the effect of TIP, let the tax rate be t on wages in excess of W_0 and assume that the receipts from the tax are returned to employers at a rate s of the total wage bill ($t > s$). The cost to the firm of employing a worker is no longer W but is

$$W + (W - W_0)t - sW = W(1 + t - s) - tW_0$$

so that (3.6) becomes

$$E = a - b(1 + t - s)W + btW_0 \tag{3.11}$$

and the maximum is now when

$$W = \frac{a + btW_0}{2b(1 + t - s)} \tag{3.12}$$

This can be simplified by noting that for the economy as a whole the tax proceeds equal the tax rebate so

$$t(W - W_0) = sW$$

and substitution for W_0 in (3.12) gives

$$W = \frac{a}{b(2 + t - s)} \tag{3.13}$$

$$E = \frac{a(1 + t - s)}{2 + t - s}. \tag{3.14}$$

By comparison of (3.14) and (3.9) the effect of the TIP is to increase employment because

$$\frac{1 + t - s}{2 + t - s} > \frac{1}{2}$$

This can also be seen by considering the graph of W against E (see Figure 3.1). From (3.6) the original demand curve is DD and with the TIP the new one is $D'D'$ from (3.11). The new optimal position is at P' where employment is higher and real wages lower than without TIP.

Jackman and Layard point out that this analysis does not allow for the consequences of a wage increase now on the tax payable next period. In taking account of this they make the simplifying assumptions that the norm, W_0 is zero and there is no productivity growth. In period j the tax paid per worker is

$$t(W_j - W_{j-1}) - sW_j$$

and so from (3.6) employment is

$$E_j = a - b((1 + t - s)W_j - tW_{j-1}) \tag{3.15}$$

The unions maximise the discounted wage bill

$$\sum E_j W_j (1 - \delta)^j$$

for $j = 1$ to ∞ subject to (3.15). Maximising and using the budget balance gives

$$W_j = \frac{a - btW_{j-1} + (1 - \delta)btW_{j+1}}{2b} \tag{3.16}$$

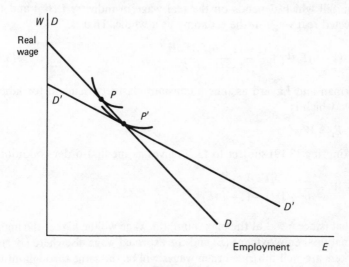

Figure 3.1

In the steady state, wages are a constant so

$$W = \frac{a}{b(2 + \delta t)} \tag{3.17}$$

and the employment rate is

$$E = \frac{a + a\delta t}{2 + \delta t} \tag{3.18}$$

which is greater than the level of employment without TIP given by (3.9). Thus the effect of the TIP is to reduce the level of unemployment.

The above model ignores the influence of the general economic climate on wage settlements. Jackman and Layard (1982) pp. 234–6 present a more general model in which the unions take account of whether their non-employed members are likely to be employed elsewhere. It is assumed that in each period firms hire a constant proportion $\theta\,(0 < \theta < 1)$ of their workers from outside their industry. Let E_i be the employment rate in industry i. For workers associated with industry i the probability of employment in industry i is $(1 - \theta)E_i$ and the probability of employment elsewhere is

$$\frac{(1 - (1 - \theta)E_i)E\theta}{1 - E(1 - \theta)}$$

where E is the national employment rate. The union maximises the real wage bill which depends on the real wage in industry i (W_i) and the expected real wage in the economy as a whole. That is,

$$(1 - \theta)E_iW_i + \frac{(1 - (1 - \theta)E_i)E\theta W^e}{1 - (1 - \theta)E} \tag{3.19}$$

Jackman and Layard assume a constant elasticity demand for labour curve which is

$$E_i = W_i^{-\eta} \tag{3.20}$$

Maximising (3.19) subject to (3.20) gives as the first-order condition

$$W_i = \frac{\eta E\theta W^e}{(\eta - 1)(1 - (1 - \theta)E)} \tag{3.21}$$

so that (since $\eta > 1$ at the maximum) the wage will be higher the higher are national employment (E) and the expected wage elsewhere (W^e). If workers are well-informed then wages will be the same throughout the economy with

$$W_i = W^e$$

so that from (3.21),

$$E = \frac{\eta - 1}{\eta - 1 + \theta} \tag{3.22}$$

and unemployment is

$$1 - E = \frac{\theta}{\eta - 1 + \theta} \tag{3.23}$$

Turning next to the effects of a TIP, Jackman and Layard consider a tax on the wage bill of firms paying wages in excess of W_O, with a negative tax for wages below W_O. The proceeds of the tax are returned to firms at a rate s on their total wage bill. All firms are assumed to pay a tax per worker of $t(W - W_O)$ and receive a rebate sW where, *ex post*,

$$t(W - W_O) = sW$$

The demand function (3.20) is now, for the industry,

$$E = (W(1 + t - s) - tW_O)^{-\eta} \tag{3.24}$$

and since E_i and W_i in (3.19) are replaced by E and W the new maximand is

$$(1 - \theta)EW + \theta EW^e \tag{3.25}$$

Maximising (3.25) subject to (3.24) gives

$$W = \frac{\eta(1 + t - s)E\theta W^e}{(\eta(1 + t - s) - 1)(1 - E(1 - \theta))} \tag{3.26}$$

and setting W to W^e gives an employment rate

$$E = \frac{\eta(1 + t - s) - 1}{\eta(1 + t - s) - 1 + \theta} \tag{3.27}$$

which is higher than (3.22) if $t > s$.

This model can be linked to the Phillips curve by taking (3.26) in logs to give

$$\ln W = \ln\left(\frac{\eta(1 + t - s)}{\eta(1 + t - s) - 1}\right) + \ln\left(\frac{E\theta}{1 - E(1 - \theta)}\right) + \ln W^e$$

Subtracting the previous period's wage gives

$$\dot{W} = f_1(\eta, t, s) + f_2(E) + \dot{W}^e \qquad (3.28)$$

where $\dot{W}^e$ is $\ln W^e - \ln W_{-i}$. Here the change in real wages is related to employment, and it can be transformed to a standard Phillips curve by adding the expected change in prices to each side and setting $\dot{W}^e$ to a constant. The non-accelerating inflation rate of unemployment (NAIRU) is found from (3.29) as

$$0 = f_1(\eta, t, s) + f_2(E) \qquad (3.29)$$

by setting actual equal to expected real wages. Thus the equilibrium level of unemployment depends on t. Layard (1982) explains that the inflation tax makes the effective demand curve faced by the unions more elastic. The result of the TIP is to reduce the union's monopoly power.

The second model proposed by Layard is an industry with one firm and one union in bilateral bargaining. In this case there is no satisfactory model to explain the outcome. The actual wage increase agreed will depend on the 'push' of the union and the 'resistance' of the employer. The market situation is illustrated in Figure 3.2 where the feasible area for a solution is shaded: the relative strengths of the parties will determine the actual values of W and E. In this situation Layard argues that the introduction of a TIP will strengthen the employer's resolve

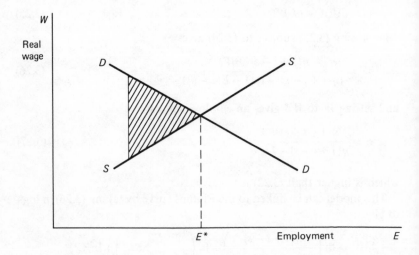

Figure 3.2

against the union, with the result that a lower wage settlement will be agreed.

The third model considered by Layard is where there is competition between firms for workers and neither side is organised. Firms can only get more workers by raising wages. In the short run, firms set wages but the adjustment to a competitive equilibrium means the monopsony power does not last. This model allows unemployment and vacancies to co-exist. The introduction of a TIP gives each firm an incentive to pay lower real wages which results in vacancies and hence lower unemployment.

3.4 CRITICISMS OF LAYARD'S MODELS OF TIP

In this section we consider criticisms of Layard's theoretical models of the effects of TIP and defer discussion of more general practical problems to section 3.5. Minford and Peel (1982) point out three features of Layard's approach which they question. First, there is no theoretical justification for including target real-wage growth in the Phillips curve (3.3). The suggestion that it results from unions and workers reacting slowly to unemployment is not satisfactory. Also, if it is a variable rather than a constant, some discussion of what determines its value is needed. Secondly, Layard does not link the three models of industry behaviour with the macroeconomic Phillips curve. The effect of the TIP is assumed to subtract a constant from the right hand side of (3.2), but how this arises from the labour market models is not stated. Thirdly, Layard relies on expectations being 'adaptive' (see, for example, Holden, Peel and Thompson, 1985) so that behaviour is essentially backward-looking rather than rational.

Minford and Peel accept that, at first sight, in Jackman and Layard's model of a strong union facing a competitive industry, TIP reduces the monopoly power of the union resulting in a lower real wage and higher employment than in the absence of TIP. However, since the tax is on the rate of change of real wages while the subsidy is on the level of the wage bill it is clear that a generalised multi-period model is required rather than a static single-period one. The analysis is therefore incomplete.

For the model of bilateral bargaining with one firm and one union, the effect of the TIP is claimed to be a lower wage settlement. Minford and Peel point out that while this may be so the resulting employment level could be above or below that agreed in the absence of the tax. In particular, if bilateral bargaining results in a settlement at the full employment level (E^* in Figure 3.2), the TIP would result in a lower level of employment. Thus with this model the tax is not necessarily beneficial.

The third model discussed by Layard assumes that neither workers nor firms are organised and that firms can only get more workers by raising wages. Since the TIP includes a subsidy to balance the tax, for the 'typical' firm the TIP has no effect. Where a firm is in a fast-growing industry, however, the tax payments would exceed the subsidy so the demand for labour would be reduced. Conversely, slow-growing industries would benefit from the subsidy and their demand for labour would increase. Whether the aggregate demand for labour would be increased is not clear. What is apparent is that there would be a re-distribution of employment from fast-growing to slow-growing industries so that social welfare would be lower (see Sargent, 1979, pp. 377–8).

Minford and Peel conclude that Layard's proposal can be regarded as a supply-side measure which attempts to reduce union monopoly power and so increase the equilibrium employment level. As its effects in the three models discussed are, at best, ambiguous they suggest that legislation may be a better way of dealing with union power.

3.5 PROBLEMS WITH AN EMPLOYER PENALTY TIP

There are many problems with the simple employer penalty TIP as outlined above. These have been reviewed by several researchers including Dildine and Sunley (1978), Slitor (1979) and Bosanquet (1983). First we will examine the implications of not having full coverage of all parts of the economy. This is usually accepted as being desirable on administrative grounds. In the USA, restricting coverage to firms with more than 100 employees eliminates 99 per cent of businesses but still includes more than 60 per cent of employment. In the UK a similar restriction would mean that fewer than 20 000 companies would be included, instead of the almost one million involved in the income tax system. By excluding small firms enormous savings in keeping records, reporting and monitoring will be obtained. Also likely to be excluded are new firms, where there is no baseline for wage increases, and unincorporated businesses such as partnerships or proprietorships, where income is partly a return on capital. The exclusion of some businesses from the effects of TIP will distort the behaviour of the market. Those businesses excluded are free to choose the combination of wages, prices and output which maximises their net profits. If the TIP is effective then unless the value of the TIP multiplier (m) is selected carefully, the outcome will be different from the free market solution and there will be a loss of efficiency in the economy. This has to be balanced against any gains attributable to the introduction of a TIP.

The second problem with the employer penalty TIP arises where the penalty applies to profits. This has implications for companies not paying profits tax and for resource allocation. Dildine and Sunley point out that in 1973, 56 per cent of corporate taxpayers paid no federal income tax and so would be unaffected by a TIP based on a profits tax surcharge. Some of these firms are running at a loss, while others benefit from tax credits. One way round this is to apply the tax to income, rather than profits, or to wage costs or prices. These will be considered along with resource allocation questions.

Any tax affects resource allocation since it changes the return to an activity. For a full discussion of the effects of taxes on profits, payroll or prices see Musgrave and Musgrave (1980). In the case of a tax on net profits of the corporate sector, if the firm has a monopoly in the product market and is maximising profits before the TIP surcharge is imposed, there will be no change in the level of output and price. The tax cannot be passed on to the consumer and so must be absorbed by the producer. However, if the firm does not maximise profits but exercises market power, or if the firm is not a monopolist, part of the tax may be passed on to consumers or wage earners depending on the particular circumstances of the market. Similarly, taxes on (gross) company income, wage costs or prices may be passed on to consumers or employees in whole or in part, according to market conditions. It is difficult to predict the precise effects of these taxes without detailed information about the market situation.

The third problem with this type of TIP is the treatment of contracts entered into before the TIP has been imposed. If there is prolonged discussion about introducing any form of incomes policy employers and unions will act quickly to reach agreement on increases before the incomes policy has effect. When contracts can apply for up to three years special rules are needed: it seems unfair for companies to be penalised under TIP for freely-reached agreements dated before the introduction of TIP.

A fourth problem for a permanent or long-run TIP occurs because a wage increase agreed now has implications for the level of wages in the future. Consider the effects of the TIP on two firms over two years starting with a wage level of 100 initially. Firm A reaches a settlement equal to the norm of 5 per cent, say, so wages are 105. Firm B exceeds the norm, agrees an increase of 10 per cent to 110 and pays a tax penalty in the first year. In the second year each firm settles at the new norm of 4 per cent. The resulting wages are 109.2 for firm A and 114.4 for firm B, showing that employees in B benefit in year 2 for not complying with the TIP in year 1. Of course there are cost, labour supply and product demand implications also, but the important point is that once an increase is given there is a higher baseline for future increases.

The fifth problem with the introduction of TIP is the choice of unit of accounting for the wages variable. For example, should the unit for a conglomerate be a single plant, a division or the whole group? It will be advantageous to any firm likely to suffer under the TIP if the accounting unit were large so that those employees settling at or below the norm bring down the average percentage increase of those receiving excessive settlements. Another accounting problem concerns the treatment of exports: since the TIP is concerned with domestic costs, should their contribution to profits be penalised? Firms which merge or acquire subsidiaries will also need careful treatment because of difficulties in defining the unit for accounting purposes. In some cases it may be appropriate to use the previous year's wages as the base for wage increases.

The next problem is the measurement of wage increases. Wallich and Weintraub (1971) suggest four alternatives: (a) total wages, bonuses, salaries, fringe benefits etc. divided by the number of employees on a particular date; (b) as (a) but divided by the daily average number of employees; (c) as (a) but divided by man-hours worked adjusted for overtime; (d) total wage and related payments in each job classification divided by the man-hours worked and combined into a weighted index of wage increases. Changes in the composition of the workforce could be manipulated to reduce the average increase in wage costs. For example the replacement of a highly paid employee by a lower paid one will reduce the wage bill. It is not clear that this is a problem if the TIP is long-term since the benefit would only be available for one year. Layard's proposal to use average hourly earnings per worker overcomes this problem.

The seventh problem is the choice of the norm. By design this is not a product of the market system and so it has to be determined by policy-makers.

3.6 VARIATIONS ON EMPLOYER TIPS

The original proposal by Wallich and Weintraub (1971) for a TIP raised much interest in the literature and various suggestions have been made for improving the basic model. While these have generally been aimed at controlling cost–push inflation they still have some relevance when the purpose of the TIP is to reduce the natural rate of unemployment

Seidman (1978) suggests that a weakness of the basic model outlined in section 3.1 is that there is no incentive to firms to reach settlements below the norm. He proposes a 'reward' TIP whereby firms benefit by paying less tax if the wage increase is below the norm. That is, the tax rate is

$$t_i = b - m(n - w_i) \quad \text{for } w_i < n$$
$$= b \quad \text{for } w_i > n$$

This can be treated as an alternative to (3.1) or can be combined with (3.1) to give a penalty-reward TIP with

$$t_i = b + m(w_i - n)$$

so that t_i varies with the settlement level. Seidman discusses some of the implications. Here we simply note that whereas with a penalty TIP firms will be glad to be exempt, whenever a reward is included firms may prefer to be included, resulting in increased administrative costs.

Another variation considered by Seidman (1978) (and also Seidman (1976)) is the employee TIP, in which the tax rate affected is that of the employee rather than the employer. Again it can include either penalties or rewards or both. An example of how this might work is given by Okun (1977). He suggested that for 1978 firms which agreed to hold the rate of wage increases for employees to below 6 per cent and the average increase in prices to below 4 per cent would receive a 5 per cent rebate on income tax liabilities on profits. Employees would receive a tax rebate of 1.5 per cent of their wages, with a ceiling of $225 per person. Layard (1982) rejects the imposition of penalties on employees on the grounds that they would provoke 'impossible political opposition' (p. 224).

Lerner (1978) points out that the weakness of penalty and/or reward TIPs is the uncertainty of how strong to make the tax incentives. He proposes that the government should issue 'wage increase permits' to employers in proportion to their total wage bill. If productivity is expected to rise on average by 3 per cent then, for each $1000 of wage bill, a permit allowing a $30 increase would be allocated. These permits would be bought and sold so that their price could be determined in the market. Lerner discusses some of the details of the scheme.

In a later version of the same idea, Lerner and Colander (1980) suggest a 'market anti-inflation plan' which rather than having wage increase permits would have 'anti-inflation credits' based on the net sales or value added of a firm. These would operate in a similar way to the wage increase permits.

As yet a complete tax-based incomes policy has not been introduced in a major economy. However, as noted in Chapter 1, section 1.4, President Carter proposed in October 1978 a real-wage insurance (RWI) scheme for the USA which had some of the characteristics of TIP. The scheme is discussed by, for example Nordhaus (1981) and Pencavel (1981), and involved a promise by the Federal Government that each employee group which accepted wage rises of up to 7 per cent would receive a tax credit if the consumer price index rose by more than 7 per cent. The value of the tax credit would be the excess of the actual inflation rate over 7 per cent, up to a maximum of 3 per cent, and applied to wages up to a limit of $20000 per job. That is, for eligible units,

$$t = b - (p - 7) \quad \text{for } 7 < p < 10$$

where t = tax rate
b = base rate of tax on labour income
p = actual rate of change of consumer price index

and all figures are percentages. Thus the emphasis was on a reward for accepting wage restraint if inflation continues at a high level. This avoids all the problems of trying to restrain prices. With a reward rather than a penalty it benefits from not being a tax and also from being thought of as 'fair': those who co-operate in wage restraint receive a bonus if inflation is higher than expected. Another advantage of the scheme was that if accepted it would have been relatively simple to operate and therefore had looked as though it might be a success. The insurance aspect was thought to be attractive to risk-averse workers but it meant that the cost of the scheme was not known in advance. However, Nordhaus estimates that if 50 per cent of workers qualify, with average earnings of $12000 then every point of inflation over 7 per cent costs $6 billion so the total cost could exceed $20 billion. Rather than try to find the possible cost, the Budget Committees of the Congress shelved RWI. This suggests that a future scheme should involve penalties as well as rewards and should even be self-balancing with the penalties and rewards being equal. Two further considerations are that individuals who would have received wage increases below 7 per cent in the absence of RWI would still benefit from it, and if the consumer price index rises because non-labour costs rise, workers are still compensated for the increase.

In the United Kingdom the Social Contract of 1974–9 (see Chapter 1, section 1.3) also included some aspects of a TIP. For example in the budget in April 1976, personal income tax cuts were proposed which would only be operational if the trade unions accepted an incomes policy with a norm of 3 per cent.

3.7 TIP AND MACROECONOMIC STABILITY

Several researchers including Seidman (1978), Peel (1979) and Scarth (1983) have examined the implications of the various forms of TIP for macroeconomic stability. Here we follow the work of Scarth who presents a simple macroeconomic model which is intended to represent the views of advocates of TIPs since it allows a 'wage–wage' or 'wage–price' view of inflation with adaptive rather than rational expectations.

Before developing the formal model we will outline the principles and the results. Changes in inflation are determined by the rate of monetary expansion while the rate of change of wages depends on the level of excess demand and previously agreed wage controls. Without a TIP the model is stable, so that following a shock to one of the exogenous variables it returns to its long-run equilibrium position. With an employee-penalty TIP the model becomes unstable but with an employer-penalty TIP the model remains stable.

The detailed model is now considered. The first equation is a dynamic version of marginal cost equals marginal revenue, assuming constant labour productivity

$$p = w + \dot{v} \tag{3.30}$$

where p = percentage change in product prices
w = percentage change in money wages
$\dot{v}$ = percentage change in payroll taxes

Next, Scarth recognises that some wage contracts cover several periods and if α is the proportion of contracts which are negotiated in every period then the current change in money wages can be written

$$w = \alpha x + (1 - \alpha) z \tag{3.31}$$

where x = percentage change in wages contracted in the current period
z = percentage change of the index of all previously contracted wages.

Now the value of z will be determined by all previous contracts, that is by past values of x. If, as the length of contract increases, the number of multi-period contracts declines geometrically we have

$$z = \phi x_{-1} + (1-\phi)\,\phi x_{-2} + (1-\phi)^2\,\phi x_{t-3} + \ldots$$

and using the Koyck transformation

$$z - (1-\phi)\,z_{-1} = \phi x_{-1}$$
$$\text{or,}\quad z - z_{-1} = \phi(x_{-1} - z_{-1}) \tag{3.32}$$

We can also rewrite (3.31) as

$$w - z = \alpha(x - z) \tag{3.33}$$

and using this in (3.32) gives

$$z - z_{-1} = \lambda(w_{-1} - z_{-1}) \tag{3.34}$$

where $\lambda = \phi/\alpha$.

The continuous time equivalent of (3.34) is

$$\dot{z} = \lambda(w - z) \tag{3.35}$$

In order to determine x, the percentage change in wages agreed in the current period, Scarth proposes

$$x = kg + (1-k)[\beta y + z - \gamma\dot{u} - (1-\gamma)\dot{v}] \tag{3.36}$$

where g = policy determined inflation norm (exogenous)
  y = excess of the logarithm of national output over the logarithm of its natural value
  u = logarithm of one minus the personal income tax rate
  v = logarithm of one plus the payroll tax rate levied on firms
  k = constant reflecting the direct effect of TIP on wage settlements
  β = positive constant.

This equation can best be understood by considering different values of k. If $k = 1$ the value of x is g so that this corresponds to a strong TIP which forces all current settlements to meet the norm. If $k = 0$ then g has no effect and the TIP is irrelevant. In this case (3.36) reduces to a standard Phillips curve with y as the excess demand measure, z is the influence of existing contracts and the effects of tax changes on wage settlements are given by $\dot{u}$ and $\dot{v}$. The final equation defines aggregate demand and is

$$\dot{y} = c(m - p) \tag{3.37}$$

where m = percentage change in nominal money supply (exogenous) which is the time derivative of the relationship between the logarithm of output and the logarithm of the real money stock. Scarth assumes a floating exchange rate, perfect capital mobility and no speculation in the foreign exchange market so that, for a small economy, the interest rate is exogenous and tax changes have no effect on demand. The model therefore consists of (3.30), (3.31), (3.35), (3.36), (3.37) plus a TIP equation. Three versions of TIP are presented and in each case tax rates equal a normal value with an adjustment if the wages or prices variable exceeds or falls short of the norm.

Before examining the effects of the different forms of TIP we will consider the stability of the model without a TIP. This means that k, $\dot{u}$ and $\dot{v}$ are all zero and the five equations are

$$p = w \tag{3.38}$$

$$w = \alpha x + (1 - \alpha)z \tag{3.39}$$

$$\dot{z} = \lambda(w - z) \tag{3.40}$$

$$x = \beta y + z \tag{3.41}$$

$$\dot{y} = c(m - p) \tag{3.42}$$

Using (3.38), (3.39) and (3.41) to eliminate p, w and x gives

$$\dot{z} = \alpha\beta\lambda y$$

$$\dot{y} = -cz - \alpha\beta cy + cm$$

and these can be written

$$\begin{bmatrix} \dot{z} \\ \dot{y} \end{bmatrix} = \begin{bmatrix} o & \alpha\beta\lambda \\ -c & -\alpha\beta c \end{bmatrix} \begin{bmatrix} z \\ y \end{bmatrix} + \begin{bmatrix} o \\ cm \end{bmatrix}.$$

Following Baumol (1959) p. 366 for stability the first matrix on the right hand side, **B**, say, must have a negative trace and a determinant with sign $(-1)^n$ where n is the number of equations. Here

Trace **B** $= -\alpha\beta c < 0$

Det **B** $= \alpha\beta\lambda c > 0$

and so the system without a TIP is stable.

The first TIP equation Scarth considers is

$$u = u^* - h(w - g) \tag{3.43}$$

where $u^* = $ normal value of u

and this is an employee TIP with the income tax rate varying with the wage settlement. (Scarth points out that replacing w by x does not affect the results here.) In this case $\dot{v}$ is set to zero in the model and the resulting equations are (3.38), (3.39), (3.40), (3.42), (3.43) and (3.36) adjusted for $\dot{v}$. Scarth shows that this system violates one of the necessary conditions for stability. Therefore if an employee TIP of this form is applied to a stable system the system becomes unstable. Thus this version of TIP is not recommended.

The second version of TIP is

$$v = v^* + h(p - g)$$

where $v^* = $ normal value of v

This is an employer TIP based on payroll tax and depending on price changes. Again this results in the system becoming unstable and so is not recommended.

The final version of TIP is

$$v = v^* + h(w - g)$$

which is an employer TIP based on payroll tax and depending on wage changes. In this case Scarth finds that the model converges so that this form of TIP may be worthwhile.

The conclusion from this analysis is that, from the examination of a simple macroeconomic model which is stable in the absence of TIP, the imposition of either an employer TIP based on price increases or an employee TIP based on wage increases makes the model unstable, and the only form of TIP which is worth further consideration is an employer TIP based on wage increases.

3.8 THE FUTURE OF TIP

The original advocates of TIP assumed that inflation was of the cost–push variety and they saw the TIP as a means of influencing the behaviour of unions and firms. More recently, economists who accept that the rate of inflation is determined by monetary expansion have argued that a TIP, by changing the nature of the constraints facing firms or unions, can influence the optimal real-wage/employment decision. Thus the TIP can be seen as a means of reducing the natural rate of unemployment. In a variety of models Layard and Jackman have shown that favourable employment consequences follow from the use of a TIP. We accept that in principle this could be the case. The objections to a TIP are that the administrative and other distortionary effects that occur when the tax is implemented could outweigh any favourable employment effects. However, a TIP is likely to be more popular but possibly less distortionary than a conventional incomes policy (see also Chapter 6). In the absence of any desire to legislate away union monopoly power, TIPs are an interesting candidate for dealing with this problem.

4 Final Offer Arbitration

4.1 INTRODUCTION

In Chapter 3 we considered variations on traditional incomes policies with enforcement being achieved by tax-based penalties or rewards. In this chapter we turn to another variation based on compulsory arbitration. Most of the literature concerning Final Offer Arbitration – i.e. arbitration based on the final offers of the parties – is found within the context of the subject of industrial relations but Meade (1982 and 1985) has advocated a modified version of final offer arbitration as part of a general macroeconomic strategy directed towards the alleviation of the current problem of stagflation (i.e. the simultaneous occurrence of high rates of inflation and unemployment). The plan of this chapter is as follows: in sections 4.2 and 4.3, we examine the roles of compulsory arbitration and final offer arbitration in order to set the framework within which Meade's proposal is based. In section 4.4 we consider in more detail the nature of the Meade proposal within the macroeconomic context and in section 4.5 discuss some criticisms levied against this strategy. Our conclusions are presented in section 4.6 and, in the appendix to this chapter, we include mathematical demonstrations of the main results described intuitively in section 4.2.

4.2 COMPULSORY ARBITRATION

Within the context of free collective bargaining a strike is generally considered as a means of imposing a cost of failure to agree on the other party to the negotiations. As pointed out by Farber and Katz (1979), the costs arising from a strike create a contract zone of potential settlements which each party considers superior to the strike outcome. In other words, the parties are willing to sacrifice some gains implicit in their claim/offer in order to avoid the cost of a strike. As such the potential existence of a strike provides an incentive to both parties to reach agreement – so that Hicks (1963) for example argues that most strikes probably result from faulty negotiations.

A simple diagrammatic demonstration of the existence of a contract zone is shown in Figure 4.1. W_u is the wage claimed by the union and W_e

the wage offered by the employer. For simplicity we assume that the costs of a strike are a fixed amount per worker and are borne equally by both parties (say equal to AB); then $W'_u (= W_u - AB)$ is the lowest wage the union would settle for in negotiations. Conversely $W'_e (W_e + AB)$ is the highest wage the employer would offer in negotiations. The shaded area between W_u and W_e represents the contract zone in which the outcome is preferred by both parties to a strike.

We now look at the role played by compulsory arbitration within the context of the industrial relations environment. A variety of different forms of compulsory arbitration exist but in quite general terms their common feature is the prohibition of strikes and lock-outs. Consequently the choice open to the parties is either to agree or go to arbitration. Generally compulsory arbitration is discussed with reference to public sector employees. Feuille (1979) argues that justification for the denial to public sector employees of the right to strike is normally based on three premises. First, the government is elected by the general public and therefore represents the 'general will' and should not be subject to pressure tactics from individual groups of workers. Secondly, public sector services are usually offered on a monopolistic basis which endows the unions with large and unfair bargaining power. Thirdly, public sector strikes hurt the general public (the 'essential service argument'). Clearly these arguments are, to say the least, controversial but, nevertheless, they are frequently used in the media to justify 'non-strike' regulations for 'essential public services'. The *quid pro quo* for the

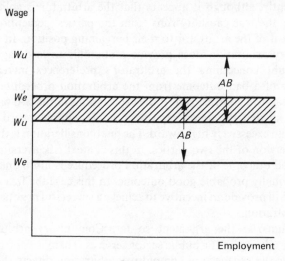

Figure 4.1

loss of the right to strike is the gain of the right to refer the dispute to a tribunal whose award is binding on both parties. Such agreements are not uncommon for state employees in the USA and other countries.

The next consideration to be examined is whether compulsory arbitration creates an incentive for the parties to reach a settlement similar to that provided by potential strikes; in other words, does the existence of compulsory arbitration lead to the existence of a contract zone. The incentive to reach an agreement is provided by four factors: 1. the costs of arbitration, 2. the arbitrator's behaviour, 3. the uncertainty concerning the arbitration award and 4. the degree of risk aversion of both parties. Clearly the costs of going to arbitration provide a stimulus directed towards a negotiated settlement in precisely the same manner as that provided by the costs of a strike. Nevertheless these costs are likely to be of a much smaller magnitude and are consequently ignored in subsequent discussion. The behaviour of the arbitrator is a more controversial factor. If the arbitrator merely splits the difference between the two claims, then there is no incentive for the parties to reach agreement. In fact the two parties are stimulated towards the adoption of extreme positions in an attempt to obtain an award favourable to themselves. This would result in 'the chilling of bargaining and excessive reliance on arbitration procedure' (Farber, 1981, p. 70). On the other hand if, as Farber argues, the arbitrator has his own ideas of what constitutes a fair result, then the parties are likely to set their offers around their perception of the arbitrator's potential award. Consequently, although it appears that the arbitrator is splitting the difference, the true causality runs from the parties' perception of the likely award of the arbitrator to their bargaining position. In this case compulsory arbitration does provide a stimulus towards agreement. Next, doubt concerning the arbitrator's preferences increases the possibility of a bad outcome from the arbitration procedure. This is likely to lead to a contract zone if the expectations of the two parties are divergent so that the union expects an adversely low award and the employer an excessively high award. The final consideration is the degree of risk aversion of the two parties. In this context risk aversion occurs when a bad outcome of the arbitration procedure is more unattractive than an equally probable good outcome. In this case the fear of a bad outcome will provide an incentive to achieve a successful negotiation and avoid arbitration.

To summarise the argument so far. Compulsory arbitration is frequently advocated for public sector services. There is controversy as to whether the existence of compulsory arbitration directs the parties towards a negotiated settlement. It is within this context that Final Offer Arbitration was advocated by Stevens (1966) as a means of overcoming the alleged reluctance of the parties to negotiate a settlement.

4.3 FINAL OFFER ARBITRATION

Final Offer Arbitration (FOA) differs from normal arbitration in that the choices open to the arbitrator are rigorously constrained. The arbitrator can award either the last claim by the union *or* the last offer of the employer. There is to be no compromise between these two. The advantage claimed for this type of arbitration is that it should provide an incentive for both parties to moderate their positions since it is known that, if either party adopts an extreme position, the arbitrator will award the other party's claim/offer. In other words, each party believes that a concession will increase the probability of the arbitrator selecting its offer so that each party will assess the loss of utility entailed by the concession against the gain in utility through the increased probability of acceptance of the party's new position by the arbitrator. The existence of a contract zone will also be influenced by the same factors discussed earlier for normal arbitration; i.e. the arbitrator's behaviour and uncertainty concerning the likely outcome, and the degree of risk aversion present. FOA could fail to produce a contract zone if either 1. both parties were risk lovers or risk neutral or 2. there are divergent expectations about the arbitration outcome. If both parties were optimistic about the outcome (note earlier we considered the case when both parties were pessimistic) then each party may prefer arbitration to the alternative of offering concessions in the negotiations. This is likely to be a short-run situation when FOA is first introduced. In the long run, it is difficult to conceive of situations where such a bias in expectations could occur especially after experience of arbitration awards. FOA has been adopted for state employees in a number of states in the USA including Massachusetts, Michigan and Wisconsin. Also, in the UK it has been incorporated into a number of collective agreements between unions and employers, as for example in the agreement between the EEPTU and Toshiba company.

Various problems arise with respect to FOA. First, as Wood (1985) points out there are practical problems in defining precisely what constitutes the last or final offer. The normal practice is for each party to put a clear statement of his final position before the arbitrator. This may, in fact, not be the last position reached in the negotiations. A related problem may also exist if either of the parties wishes to amend their position during the arbitration procedure. Clear rules concerning these matters will have to be laid down in the agreement setting up FOA. Secondly, there is the possibility that one party may incorporate in an otherwise reasonable offer which approximates the arbitrator's preferences, one item which it is known that the other party would never concede in free negotiation. This is known in the relevant literature as a 'zinger'. The incorporation of a zinger could be due either to a deliberate act or alternatively to misjudgement. In reality, this is a particular example of a more general problem as to what happens if each offer was perceived by the other party (and the arbitrator) to be patently unjust. Thirdly, the hearings of the dispute before an arbitrator are unlikely to reveal much information about the preferences of the two parties since their concessions are related to their pre-arbitration positions and, in any case, are likely to be related to their perception of the arbitrator's preferences.

To overcome these defects, a number of suggestions have been made (see Donn, 1977). These include; 1. Repeated Offer Selection, 2. Modified Final Offer Arbitration, 3. Multiple Offer Selection and 4. Issue by Issue Arbitration. Turning first of all to Repeated Offer Selection, if the arbitrator feels that his selection of either party's offer would be grossly unfair to the other party, he would announce that both offers are unacceptable and that each party should submit a new offer. Modified Final Offer Arbitration is designed to overcome the same problem but involves the arbitrator amending one of the final offers. This is then offered to both parties as a settlement to the dispute. Provided both parties agree, the arbitrator's amended offer is then introduced as the settlement. In the absence of such agreement, the arbitrator is forced to select one of the original offers. In Multiple Final Offer Arbitration, each party submits a number of offers. The arbitrator then selects which party's set of final offers is acceptable and leaves the other party to select the precise offer which is to be implemented. For example, suppose each party submits three offers $A1$, $A2$ and $A3$; $B1$, $B2$ and $B3$ respectively. The arbitrator decides that B's offers are to be awarded and party A would then choose between $B1$, $B2$ and $B3$. The reasoning behind this scheme is that, if each party submits individual offers reflecting approximately equal utility, then the other party can maximise its own utility by selecting the most desirable offer without reducing the utility of the successful party. Finally in Issue by Issue arbitration, each party submits a list of proposals from which the arbitrator can select individual components in the award.

We have now completed the background survey of issues related to arbitration and in the following section we consider the proposal made by Meade. While this is intended for the particular industrial relations situation in the United Kingdom, the basic principles have wider applicability.

4.4 THE MEADE PROPOSAL

We would like to re-emphasise that the FOA proposal forms just one component of a general macroeconomic strategy advocated by Meade to achieve the twin targets of full employment and stable prices. Traditional Keynesian conventional wisdom has viewed the role of monetary and fiscal policy to set the level of aggregate demand so as to achieve full employment. In this framework the role of wage and price controls is to achieve stable prices. Meade proposes to reverse this ordering of targets and instruments. Monetary and fiscal policy are to be determined so as to achieve a steady growth in the level of nominal GNP and, within that growth of aggregate demand, the role of the prices and incomes policy is to achieve full employment. This policy can easily be clarified by referring to the simple quantity theory of money, i.e.

$$m + v = q + p \qquad (4.1)$$

where m = the growth of the nominal money supply
v = the growth of velocity of circulation (assumed here to be constant for ease of exposition)
q = the growth of real output
p = the growth of the price level (i.e. inflation)

Standard monetarist thought predicts causation running from m to p on the grounds that q is determined by real forces and v is stable and determined by factors other than m or q. In the Meade proposal, m would increase by say x per cent per annum and therefore any restraint in p achieved by an incomes policy would lead to a higher q and consequently employment. This leaves open the question as to what type of incomes policy would be best fitted to achieve the restraint in p. Meade argues that the traditional/centralised income policy as discussed in Chapter 2 would be inappropriate and unlikely to work. He therefore advocates the use of final offer arbitration which turns out not to be completely compulsory – Not-Quite-Compulsory Arbitration (Meade, 1982). He emphasises that the introduction of this type of policy could only be implemented if there was widespread political agreement that a change in policy of this nature was desirable. Consequently Meade argues that the following additional and supplementary policies are necessary to obtain the widespread political consensus:

1. a radical reform of the taxation/welfare benefit system so as to attain both a 'more acceptable' distribution of real national income and a more efficient method of directing resources to those in need.
2. Development of opportunities for employees to participate in decision-making within their enterprises.
3. Promotion of competition.

Within this general macroeconomic strategy the role of the incomes policy is to assist the price mechanism to allocate labour efficiently between the various industries whilst avoiding inflation. In other words relative wages should be permitted to change but within a non-inflationary environment. A detailed explanation of how the FOA incomes policy is to achieve this aim is contained in Meade (1985). First it is necessary to develop some form of consultative/co-operative machinery to determine the norm for wage increases which is compatible with the given monetary/fiscal expansion and which will produce full employment. The second strand of the strategy is the development of a permanent system of pay tribunals to settle disputes. The emphasis is on permanent rather than *ad hoc* tribunals so as to provide consistency within their awards. These tribunals would operate according to the FOA principle discussed earlier. In the absence of agreement the dispute would be referred to the tribunal who would award either the union's last claim or the employer's last offer. However, unlike the traditional FOA industrial relations literature discussed earlier, Meade proposed the award would be based on which offer/claim would be likely to lead to the greatest level of employment rather than some nebulous concept of 'fairness'. Meade qualifies this criterion by suggesting that the employment should be 'real' jobs and hence amends the criterion to maximising output so as to avoid unnecessary job creation. This is illustrated in Figure 4.2 under conditions of bilateral monopoly. The employer would prefer a wage equal to W_e whereas the union would prefer W_u. The greatest level of employment is attained at W_c. Consequently an omniscient arbitrator would make the award according to which of the two parties' position was nearer W_c.

Meade advocates that the presumption of the arbitration should be in favour of the employee's last claim unless the employer can show beyond reasonable doubt that their offer meets the following three criteria:

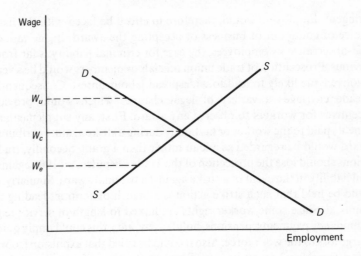

Figure 4.2

1. In the long run output would be sustainable at a higher level.
2. The offer did not imply a rate of increase less than the agreed norm by *x* per cent (Meade quotes a figure of 3 percentage points).
3. Similar to (2) above, the offer did not imply a pay relativity of more than *y* per cent less than the previous 5 years average (again a figure of 3 percentage points is quoted).

Criteria (2) and (3) are incorporated to limit movements in relative wages on the grounds that large abrupt changes would be undesirable in the short run but changes are necessary in the long run. Meade argues that this system could easily be extended to the public sector provided cash limits are announced so as to provide an indication of the measure of demand for a particular service. Against the background of the established norm, the tribunal would, in order to accept the employer's offer, have to be certain that it would attract sufficient employment to provide the service at a higher level than would be the case implicit in the employees' claim. In addition points (2) and (3) above would also apply.

The final factor to be discussed in connection with the role of FOA is what means are to be used to ensure compliance with the scheme. Meade expects that it would be illegal for an employer to employ workers except at the wage awarded by the tribunal. Non-compliance would then be a criminal offence and the penalties for non-observance would be stringent. Employers would, therefore in effect, be faced with the hard choice of going out of business or accepting the award. In the case of non-observance by employees, the case for criminal liability is far from obvious. Prosecution of trade union officials or members would be a very emotive issue likely to lead to widespread labour unrest. Consequently Meade envisages a variety of legal changes which would provide incentives for workers to observe any award. First, any supplementary benefits paid to the worker or his family during a strike against a tribunal award would be regarded as a loan rather than a grant. Secondly, trade unions should lose the protection of the Trade Disputes Act 1906 against civil liability in the event of a strike against a tribunal award. Similarly, it could be held that such strike action is a breach of contract leading to dismissal. Since some worker rights are linked to length of service (e.g. redundancy payments, pensions, holiday pay, etc.), this could imply quite a large loss to the work force. Also it could be ruled that expulsion from a union for refusal to strike was illegal in the case of a strike against acceptance of the tribunal award. This would leave the relevant union open to legal action by any aggrieved worker. Finally it is possible to make an individual striker liable for damages caused by his actions. These changes in the law would be designed to persuade workers that acceptance of the award was the best policy open to them. Whether they would be successful in practice is an open question.

4.5 CRITIQUE OF THE MEADE PROPOSAL

Apart from the general problems associated with FOA, a number of queries can be raised in connection with the strategy discussed in section 4.4. First, there is the very real problem that such a policy would not be acceptable to either (or both) employers or employees. In the absence of the widespread political consensus sought by Meade, it seems doubtful whether the sanctions discussed above are sufficiently practical to secure compliance. This point is of course recognised by Meade and is the reason for the inclusion of the supplementary policies discussed earlier. In addition the presumption in favour of the employees' claim is designed to compensate employees for their proposed loss of rights involved when sanctions are imposed in the case of non-observance.

A second problem concerns the possibility of employers and employees freely negotiating wage increases above the norm. Arbitration only applies in the case of a dispute. In order to counteract this problem Meade (1985) proposes the additional use of a form of a TIP on the lines outlined in the previous chapter. However, we raised doubts about the efficacy of a TIP in Chapter 3 and these would of course apply equally in the case of a TIP used in conjunction with FOA.

As in the case of a TIP, there is also the administrative problem of defining a wage increase. Any squeeze on money wage increases would inevitably lead to a growth in fringe benefits as an attempt to avoid the rigours of the pay policy. Such moves would be difficult for the authorities to monitor and to eradicate.

The role of the arbitrators is also open to question. They are required to possess a fair degree of sophisticated knowledge about the market in order to decide which offer/claim is likely to lead to the highest level of output and employment. It is not unreasonable to ask whether such knowledge exists in practice. For example any award other than W_c in Figure 4.2 leads to a lower level of employment than that reached by free collective bargaining.

Finally a more sophisticated criticism is raised by Dolton and Treble (1985). They contend that the claims made for this strategy depend on the type of model assumed for the labour market. Referring back to Figure 4.2 the result of the analysis depends on the existence of a labour supply curve. They consider two types of labour models: monopoly union and efficient bargains. Both can be demonstrated using the same diagram which Dolton and Treble take from McDonald and Solow (1981). This is shown as Figure 4.3 where W is the money wage (we are assuming constant prices again for ease of exposition) and N the level of employment within the industry. Note also we are assuming the labour input variable is numbers of workers rather than hours worked. P_1, P_2 ... represent isoprofit lines with P_2 representing a higher profit level than P_1, etc. I_1, I_2 ... are the union's indifference curves with respect to wages and employment. In the case of the monopoly union model, the union sets the wage and the firm decides the number of workers to employ at that wage. Thus employment at any wage set by the union will be at the highest point of the relevant isoprofit curve assuming profit maximisation. Consequently the line DD traces the firms demand for labour. With the criterion of promoting employment, the arbitrator would select the lower wage offer/claim which may quite reasonably be assumed to approximate to the employer's offer. In other words the arbitrator would be consistently making awards to the employer and such a bias is unlikely to promote acceptance of the arbitration scheme in the long run. If the assumption is made that the efficient bargains model holds then the converse is true and the arbitrator would consistently favour the union's claim. In this version of the efficient bargains model,

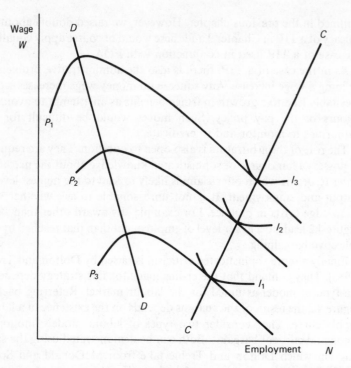

Figure 4.3

the union would be concerned with bargaining for wages and employment. Bargains would be struck at points of tangency of the union's indifference curve and the firms' isoprofit curve. The contract curve *CC* traces the set of feasible efficient bargains. Clearly in this case to raise employment the arbitrator would award the higher of the two final offers which on any reasonable criteria is likely to be the union's claim.

4.6 CONCLUSIONS

Meade's proposal is designed to assist the operation of the price mechanism. However, great reliance is placed on the role of the arbitrator and if he/she 'gets it wrong' employment is not stimulated. In practice it may be argued that the scheme is a step towards a planned economy with decisions in the labour market being undertaken by an omniscient planner. Those who believe in the free market mechanism would, no doubt, argue that a better result could be obtained by the promotion of competition within the labour markets especially as the outcome from arbitration is not certain to be better than that derived from operation of the market. In addition there are the specific problems associated with the scheme which were discussed in section 4.5. On the other hand high unemployment for any prolonged period involves high costs.

4.7 APPENDIX

In this appendix we present a more formal demonstration of the main results described intuitively in section 4.2. The general approach follows Farber (1981).

Suppose two parties are bargaining over the division of a fixed 'pie' the size of which is assumed to be 1 for simplicity. Consequently the share of each party in the award can be represented by a number ranging from 0 to 1. A process depicting an arbitration process which achieves a compromise between the two parties can be specified as:

$$A_F = aX_A + (1-a)X_B \qquad (4.2)$$

where X_A = the share to A given by A's last claim
X_B = the share to A given by B's last claim
A_F = the share given to A by the arbitrator
a defines the terms of the compromise.

Note, by definition, the corresponding shares to B are $1 - X_A$, $1 - X_B$ and $1 - A_F$ respectively.

If the arbitrator splits the difference by some constant fraction (i.e. a is a constant) then each party will have the incentive to make its offer as extreme as possible. This is easily seen by letting the utility function for A be denoted $U_A(A_F)$. Differentiating $U_A(A_F)$ with respect to X_A yields $aU'(A_F)$ which is greater than zero for all values of X_A and X_B yielding positive marginal utility. Consequently A will set X_A equal to 1 and so will demand the whole of the pie. This demonstrates the point made in section 4.2 that splitting-the-difference arbitration is likely to lead to the parties' adopting extreme positions and a 'chilling' of the bargaining procedure.

Now let us assume that the arbitrator has some concept of a fair award. This idea of equity enters into the relative weights given to X_A and X_B in the arbitration process. Such a process can be captured by the following expression:

$$a = g(A_E - 0.5[X_A + X_B]) \qquad (4.3)$$

where g is a monotonically increasing function and

$$g(0) = 0.5.$$

This function implies that if the offers are set symmetrically around the arbitrator's concept of a fair award then $a = 0.5$ and the arbitrator splits the difference. If the average offer is greater than A_E then a will be less than 0.5. This skews the award in favour of the low offer.

At this stage of the analysis, it is assumed that the parties know the arbitrator's view of an equitable award. If party A sets his last offer to maximise his utility given B's last offer, and similarly for B, then

$$\partial U_A / \partial X_A = U'_A (A_F) \partial A_F / \partial X_A = 0 \qquad (4.4)$$

$$\partial U_B / \partial X_B = -U'_B (1 - A_F) \partial A_F / \partial X_B = 0 \qquad (4.5)$$

This pair of equations constitutes a 'Nash' equilibrium in that neither party can achieve a higher expected utility by changing its offer.

Using the definition of A_F in (4.2) and that of a in (4.3) and re-arranging (4.4) and (4.5) produces:

$$0 = a - 0.5[X_A - X_B]g'(A_E - 0.5[X_A + X_B]) \qquad (4.6)$$

$$0 = (1 - 0.5a) - 0.5[X_A - X_B]g(A_E - 0.5[X_A + X_B]) \qquad (4.7)$$

It is self-evident from these equations that in equilibrium $a = (1 - a) = 0.5$ which using (4.3) implies that the average of the parties' last offers is equal to the arbitrator's view of equity, that is

$$A_E = (X_A + X_B)/2 \qquad (4.8)$$

This supports the contention in the text that although it appeared that the arbitrator is merely splitting the difference, the causality runs in the opposite direction from the arbitrator's view of equity to the parties' offers.

We now make the analysis more realistic by introducing uncertainty. This is achieved through the assumption that the parties do not know the arbitrator's view of a fair award. The arbitrator's award (A_F) in this case can be represented by:

$$A_F = (1 - b)A_E + b(X_A + X_B)/2 \qquad (4.9)$$

where b is the weight attached by the arbitrator to the position of the two parties.

The two parties attempt to maximise their expected utility given by:

$$E(U_A) = \int_0^1 U_A(A_F)f(A_E)dA_E \qquad (4.10)$$

$$E(U_B) = \int_0^1 U_B(1 - A_F)f(A_E)dA_E \qquad (4.11)$$

where $f(A_E)$ is the relative probability density function. In order to make the analysis more tractable, a particular form of probability density function is assumed. This exhibits constant absolute risk aversion and is:

$$U_A(b) = 1 - \exp(-Z_A b) \qquad (4.12)$$

$$U_B(1 - b) = 1 - \exp(-Z_B[1 - b]) \qquad (4.13)$$

where Z_A and Z_B are the absolute risk aversion parameters of the two parties. The further assumption is made that A_E is normally distributed with mean $\bar{A}_E$ and variance σ^2. Strictly speaking these assumptions are invalid for 'shares' of a pie which have a range from 0 to 1. However this objection can be overcome by making the additional assumption that the variance is small so that the mass outside the range 0 to 1 is minute. Since A_F is a linear function of A_E, $A_{F'}$ it is normally distributed with mean:

$$\bar{A}_F = (1 - b)\bar{A}_E + b([X_A + X_B]/2) \tag{4.14}$$

and variance $(1 - b)^2\sigma^2$. The final assumption made is that the parameter b is defined by:

$$b = \exp(-q[X_A - X_B]) \tag{4.15}$$

where the parameter q describes how quickly b falls as the offer of the two parties diverge. Notice that $b = 1$ if $X_A = X_B$.

Using (4.12) and (4.13), the distribution of A_F and the Laplace transform of a normally distributed random variable, the two utility functions may be approximated by:

$$E(U_A) = 1 - \exp[-Z_A A_F] + 0.5\sigma^2[1 - b]^2 Z_A^2) \tag{4.16}$$

$$E(U_B) = 1 - \exp(-Z_B[1 - A_F] + 0.5\sigma^2[1 - b]^2 Z_B^2) \tag{4.17}$$

Differentiating (4.16) and (4.17) with respect to X_A and X_B, setting the derivatives equal to zero, and using (4.15) with rearranging produces:

$$0 = (A_E - [X_A + X_B]/2 - \sigma^2(1 - b)Z_A)q + \tfrac{1}{2} \tag{4.18}$$

$$0 = (-A_E + [X_A + X_B]/2 - \sigma^2(1 - b)Z_B)q + \tfrac{1}{2} \tag{4.19}$$

These two equations define the Nash equilibrium pair of final positions.

The existence of a potential contract zone where negotiated settlements are preferred by both parties to arbitration can be obtained by comparing the utility derived from arbitration and that from a negotiated settlement. The lower level (X_L) of this contract zone is given where the share yields the same expected utility as that derived from arbitration. Any share over X_L would be acceptable to A. Conversely any share to A less than that which would yield the same expected utility to B as arbitration provides the upper limit of the contract zone (X_U). These two limits are, therefore, defined by:

$$X_L = A_F - 0.5\sigma^2(1 - b)^2 Z_A \tag{4.20}$$

$$X_U = A_F + 0.5\sigma^2(1 - b)^2 Z_B \tag{4.21}$$

Hence the size of the contract zone (CZ) is obtained by subtracting (4.20) from (4.21) to obtain:

$$CZ = 0.5\sigma^2(1 - b)^2(Z_A + Z_B) \tag{4.22}$$

The size of the contract zone is therefore inversely related to the weight the arbitrator puts on the position of the two parties. If the arbitrator is not influenced by the position of the two parties, then $b = 0$ and the contract zone is given by:

$$CZ = 0.5\sigma^2(Z_A + Z_B) \tag{4.23}$$

so that the contract zone depends entirely on σ^2 and the degree of risk aversion of the two parties.

5 Indexation

5.1 INTRODUCTION

Many of the problems that occur in wage negotiations (and in financial transactions generally) result from the fact that services or goods are to be supplied over a period of months or years and the future level of prices is unknown. One way of dealing with this is by indexation or escalator clauses whereby the value of the payment is automatically revised in line with an agreed measure of prices. An example would be a one-year wage agreement between employees and employers in which the contract includes an 'escalator clause' by which the wage rate negotiated today will be increased (or decreased) each month in line with movements in the retail price index over the coming year. In this case wages are said to be contingent on retail prices. The wide international experience of indexation agreements is summarised by Page (1975) and Beeton (1985). Their long history in Australia is discussed in Chapter 1, section 1.6 above, while in section 1.4 for the UK the Heath government's 'threshold payments' are explained.

Unlike formal incomes policies, the adoption of indexation agreements still permits variation in the negotiated wage rates in different sectors of the economy. Consequently, wages are free to move in response to differential shifts in demand and supply so that interference with the price mechanism is less than with formal incomes policies.

In this chapter we consider the role of indexation in various circumstances. Rigidities provided by the slow adjustment of expectations (i.e. the case of adaptive expectations) are discussed in section 5.2. The analysis is extended in section 5.3 and 5.4 to the situation where expectations are well-informed (i.e. the case of rational expectations) but actual wage rates may not be flexible because of wage contracts. Our results suggest that indexation may reduce the impact of monetary shocks but exaggerate the impact of real shocks. Consequently, in section 5.5 we consider whether an optimal level of indexation exists. Practical issues concerning the role of indexation are reviewed in section 5.6.

In the remainder of this chapter we shall assume for ease of exposition that, in the aggregate, inflation is caused by monetary factors. As outlined in Chapter 2, it is our belief that pure cost–push models have little empirical validity. However, for completeness we consider briefly the impact of escalator clauses in the context of cost–push models. Since, under the cost–push hypothesis, inflation is independent of output changes, the introduction of indexation will leave output (or its rate of growth) unchanged. Also, as inflation is caused by exogenous factors, the rate of wage increase will reflect both these exogenous factors and the effects of indexation. Consequently workers who are members of weak trade unions will be protected from the impact on the general price level of wage increases negotiated by members of strong trade unions. To that extent, social justice may be preserved by indexation but the overall outcome is likely to be an increase in inflation.

5.2 ADAPTIVE EXPECTATIONS

Milton Friedman (1974) puts forward a strong case for indexation. He argues that escalator clauses should be compulsory in the government sector but voluntary in the private sector, with no legal obstacles to their implementation. His rationale for their voluntary nature in the private sector is that if the government manages money responsibly so as to prevent inflation then escalator clauses will have no permanent role and will be discarded when no longer appropriate. Friedman also argues that indexation will reduce the worst effects of contractionary monetary policy on real economic variables.

The economic assumptions behind these arguments are first that inflation is a monetary phenomenon, second that agents do not suffer from money illusion and are concerned *ex ante* with the anticipated real value of economic variables and third that agents' expectations or anticipations of inflation respond slowly to a new monetary environment. This third assumption is crucial to the argument and implies that without indexation monetary changes will have a distortionary effect on the real economy.

A simple macroeconomic model (without indexation) which illustrates the points raised by Friedman is given by the following equations

$$m = m^d = m^s = p + y \tag{5.1}$$

$$w = \lambda(\log Y - \log \bar{Y}) + p^e + u \tag{5.2}$$

$$p = w \tag{5.3}$$

$$p^e = p_{-1} \tag{5.4}$$

where m^s, m^d are the proportionate rates of change of money supplied and demanded, m is their common value, Y is the level of real output, $\bar{Y}$ is the equilibrium level of real output, y is the proportional rate of change of real output ($y = \Delta \log Y$), w is the proportionate rate of change of money wages, p is the proportionate rate of change of prices, p^e is the expected proportionate rate of change of prices, λ is a positive constant, u is a random shock with an expected value of zero. Equation (5.1) is the demand for money function in which interest rates are omitted for simplicity, (5.2) is an augmented Phillips curve, (5.3) is a simple mark-up price equation and (5.4) is an adaptive expectations mechanism by which expected inflation for the period ahead equals the observed current rate of inflation. More complicated forms of adaptive expectations do not alter the substance of the analysis.

We can solve the model for p by substitution from (5.3) and (5.4) into (5.2), first differencing the resulting equation and then using (5.1) to eliminate y. This gives

$$p = \frac{1}{1+\lambda} \{2p_{-1} - p_{-2} + \lambda m - \lambda \bar{y} + u - u_{-1}\} \qquad (5.5)$$

Similarly, the solution for y is obtained by substitution from (5.3) and (5.4) into (5.2), and using the result to eliminate p from (5.1) which is then differenced twice to give

$$y = \frac{1}{1+\lambda} \{2y_{-1} - y_{-2} + m - 2m_{-1} + m_{-2} + \lambda \bar{y} - u + u_{-1}\} \qquad (5.6)$$

We now examine the effects in this model of a reduction in the rate of monetary growth (m). From (5.5) and (5.6) there is an immediate fall in both inflation and the growth of real output. This can also be seen from (5.1) where reducing m reduces p and y. Since the rate of inflation depends on output relative to equilibrium output and expected inflation, the initial impact is on output before expected inflation starts adjusting in the next period. The presence of lagged variables in (5.5) and (5.6) implies a slow movement towards the new equilibrium.

If escalator clauses are adopted then the parties to wage negotiations need no longer be concerned with expected inflation since the agreed nominal wage will adjust in line with actual inflation. To allow for full indexation, the wage equation (5.2) is replaced by

$$w = \lambda (\log Y - \log \bar{Y}) + \alpha p + (1 - \alpha)p^e + u \qquad (5.7)$$

where α is the proportion of wage contracts which include escalator clauses. If $\alpha = 1$ the term in expected inflation drops from (5.7) and real wages are related to the deviation of output from its equilibrium value. If $\alpha = 0$ then (5.2) results. Solving the new model, i.e. (5.1), (5.3), (5.4) and (5.7) as previously gives, for p,

$$p = \frac{1}{1-\alpha+\lambda}\{(1-\alpha)(2p_{-1}-p_{-2}) + \lambda m - \lambda \bar{y} + u - u_{-1}\} \tag{5.8}$$

and for y,

$$y = \frac{1}{1-\alpha+\lambda}\{(1-\alpha)(2y_{-1}-y_{-2}+m-2m_{-1}+m_{-2})$$

$$+ \lambda \bar{y} - u + u_{-1}\} \tag{5.9}$$

The effects of the escalator clauses can be seen by comparing (5.8) and (5.9) with (5.5) and (5.6). They are the same if $\alpha = 0$ (no indexed wage contracts) while if $\alpha = 1$ (all contracts are indexed) (5.8) and (5.9) reduce to

$$p = m - \bar{y} + \frac{u - u_{-1}}{\lambda} \tag{5.10}$$

$$y = \bar{y} - \frac{u - u_{-1}}{\lambda} \tag{5.11}$$

which show that output becomes independent of changes in monetary policy in this model. For the more general case where the proportion of contracts indexed is α per cent, the effects of monetary change on output are reduced relative to the non-indexed case since

$$\frac{1-\alpha}{1-\alpha+\lambda} < \frac{1}{1+\lambda}$$

Notice also that the cyclical behaviour of prices and output evident in (5.5) and (5.6) is also present with partial indexation (in (5.8) and (5.9) with $\alpha < 1$) with a modified amplitude but disappears with full indexation in (5.10) and (5.11). Thus in this simple model with a demand for money function, an augmented Phillips curve, a mark-up price equation and adaptive expectations, full indexation removes the possibility of cyclical behaviour of the economy.

More generally, if expectations are formed adaptively then indexation can insulate the real economy from monetary changes.

The above arguments lie behind Friedman's advocacy of compulsory indexation agreements in public contracts. What is less clear is why such agreements should not also be compulsory for the private sector, where they would protect private agents from the consequences of government actions. Friedman's argument that the private use of indexation agreements should be voluntary in order to promote their self destruction once governments manage monetary policy in a responsible manner seems unsatisfactory. Compulsory agreements could also be scrapped when they are no longer needed. Moreover, in the absence of government intervention, it is not clear why agents in the private sector (who Friedman assumes form their expectations adaptively) would seek voluntary indexation agreements. If they realise that their expectations are inaccurate, so that indexation is needed, surely they would abandon their adaptive mechanism and adopt a more successful approach. Such changes would tend to remove the slow adjustment of expectations to changed monetary conditions which is central to Friedman's argument for indexation. This has led to a discussion of the need for indexation when agents are assumed to have rational expectations, which is the subject of section 5.3.

Before turning to these issues we dispense with one issue raised by a number of authors including Friedman (1974) and Jackman and Klappholz (1975). This is, if contracts are to be indexed compulsorily, what price measure should be used? Among the candidates are the retail price index, the consumers' expenditure deflator and the price index of GDP at factor cost. Friedman argues that the choice of price index is important but not critical. Jackman and Klappholz, however, argue that the choice is critical and that the use of an index of retail prices is inappropriate since it is the underlying rate of inflation which matters. Therefore, the effects of relative price changes, terms of trade changes, and changes in indirect taxes and subsidies should be excluded from the index. They give the examples of Denmark and the Netherlands where indirect taxes are excluded from the price index used for purposes of indexation.

While this argument is plausible it may be irrelevant if expectations are unbiased (as with the rational expectations hypothesis). Suppose that compulsory escalation clauses are imposed by the government and linked to a price index on which agents did not base their price expectations prior to indexation. In these circumstances it seems reasonable for the negotiated nominal contracts to reflect agents' expectations of the difference over the contract period between the official index and that which agents would have used in the absence of the compulsory indexation agreement. For example, if agents expect the official index to rise by 3 per cent while their own index will rise by 10 per cent, then the negotiations over the nominal contract will involve the extra 7 per cent not covered by the official index. The only way the authorities could negate this behaviour is by limiting the value of the nominal contract, in which case this is best viewed as a conventional incomes policy.

5.3 RATIONAL EXPECTATIONS

First we will consider the effects of expectations being formed rationally on the simple macroeconomic model presented in the previous section. The assumption of rational expectations implies that the expected proportionate change in prices is both unbiased and the minimum variance predictor of all possible predictors. (See Holden, Peel and Thompson, 1985). The model, with no indexation of contracts, is

$$m = p + y \tag{5.1}$$

$$w = \lambda(\log Y - \log \bar{Y}) + p^e + u \tag{5.2}$$

$$p = w \tag{5.3}$$

with the rational expectations equation

$$p_t^e = E_{t-1} p_t \tag{5.12}$$

where the right hand side indicates the expectation of p_t formed at time $t-1$ on the basis of all available and relevant information (which includes the structural equations of this model). The model can be simplified by using the definition of y to give

$$m_t = p_t + \log Y_t - \log Y_{t-1} \tag{5.13}$$

$$p_t = \lambda(\log Y_t - \log \bar{Y}) + p_t^e + u_t \tag{5.14}$$

Taking the expectation of (5.14) gives

$$E_{t-1} p_t = \lambda(E_{t-1} \log Y_t - \log \bar{Y}) + p_t^e$$

or $\quad E_{t-1} \log Y_t = \log \bar{Y} \tag{5.15}$

by using (5.12). Taking the expectation of (5.13) gives

$$E_{t-1} m_t = E_{t-1} p_t + E_{t-1} \log Y_t - \log Y_{t-1}$$

and subtracting this from (5.13) results in

$$m_t - E_{t-1} m_t = p_t - E_{t-1} p_t + \log Y_t - E_{t-1} \log Y_t$$
$$= \lambda(\log Y_t - \log \bar{Y}) + \log Y_t - \log \bar{Y} + u_t$$

by using (5.14) and (5.15). This can be re-arranged as

$$\log Y_t - \log \bar{Y} = \frac{1}{1+\lambda} (m_t - E_{t-1} m_t - u_t) \qquad (5.16)$$

Now if expectations are rational the difference between the actual growth of the money supply (m_t) and its expectation $(E_{t-1} m_t)$ will be a random error (assuming that the authorities monetary policy is not perfectly predictable). If we let

$$m_t - E_{t-1} m_t = v_t \qquad (5.17)$$

then from (5.16),

$$\log Y_t - \log \bar{Y} = \frac{1}{1+\lambda} (v_t - u_t) \qquad (5.18)$$

and thus the variance of the deviation of the logarithm of output around the full employment level (without indexation) is

$$\text{Var}(Y_N) = \frac{1}{(1+\lambda)^2} (\sigma_v^2 + \sigma_u^2) \qquad (5.19)$$

if it is also assumed that u and v, the real and the nominal shocks, are uncorrelated. The solution for y is obtained by differencing (5.18) to give

$$y_t = \bar{y} + \frac{1}{1+\lambda} (v_t - v_{t-1} - u_t + u_{t-1}) \qquad (5.20)$$

and the solution for p is obtained by using (5.20) with (5.1) or

$$p_t = m_t - \bar{y} - \frac{1}{1+\lambda} (v_t - v_{t-1} - u_t + u_{t-1}) \qquad (5.21)$$

These solutions are similar to (5.10) and (5.11) above, which arose from full indexation with adaptive expectations. In the present case, however, there is both a real and a nominal shock (i.e. u and v respectively).

Next, assume that there is full indexation so that expected inflation in (5.2) is replaced by actual inflation to give

$$p_t = \lambda(\log Y_t - \log \bar{Y}) + p_t + u_t$$

or $\log Y_t = \log \bar{Y} - \dfrac{u_t}{\lambda}$ \qquad (5.22)

The solution for y is

$$y_t = \bar{y} - \frac{u_t - u_{t-1}}{\lambda} \qquad (5.23)$$

and that for p, using (5.1), is

$$p_t = m_t - \bar{y} + \frac{u_t - u_{t-1}}{\lambda} \tag{5.24}$$

Notice that these do not involve the nominal shock v, so that rational expectations with indexation insulates output from the effect of v. Also, (5.23) and (5.24) are the same as (5.10) and (5.11). That is, for the theoretical model outlined above, the behaviour of output and prices is the same under adaptive or rational expectations as long as there is full indexation.

From (5.22) the variance of the deviation of the logarithm of output around the full employment level (with indexation) is

$$\text{Var}(Y_I) = \frac{\sigma_u^2}{\lambda^2} \tag{5.25}$$

and by comparison with (5.19), the variance under indexation will be larger than that without indexation if

$$\frac{\sigma_u^2}{\lambda^2} > \frac{\sigma_u^2 + \sigma_v^2}{(1+\lambda)^2} \tag{5.26}$$

or $\quad \dfrac{\sigma_u^2}{\sigma_v^2} > \dfrac{\lambda^2}{1+2\lambda}$

That is, it is possible for indexation to exacerbate the effects of real shocks on the level of output. This was pointed out by Gray (1976) and Fischer (1977) and we now consider this in the context of the structural model outlined by Gray.

5.4 THE GRAY MODEL

We now consider a more complicated model, based on Gray (1976) which allows us to investigate the effects of shocks on real output. The starting point is the production function which in log-linear form is

$$\log Y = \delta \log L + u \tag{5.27}$$

where Y is the level of output, L is the level of the labour input, δ is the elasticity of real output with respect to the labour input and u is a randomly distributed real shock (with a mean of zero). By differentiation the marginal product of labour is obtained and setting this equal to the real wage rate (R or W/P) gives

$$\log L^D = -\frac{1}{1-\delta} (\log R - u) + K \qquad (5.28)$$

where K is a constant and L^D is the demand for labour. The supply of labour depends on the real wage and is given by

$$\log L^s = \phi \log R + K \qquad (5.29)$$

Initially, nominal money supply is assumed to be fixed at $\bar{M}$, and non-stochastic

$$\log M^s = \log \bar{M} \qquad (5.30)$$

and the demand for money balances is

$$\log M^D = k + \log P + \log Y \qquad (5.31)$$

where k is a constant. Equilibrium in the money market gives

$$\log M^s = \log M^D \qquad (5.32)$$

or, by substitution and using the definition of R,

$$\log \bar{M} = k + \log \frac{W}{R} + \log Y \qquad (5.33)$$

The essential feature of this model is that a one-period contract determines the nominal base wage rate (W^*) and an indexing parameter (γ) before the value of the real shock is known. The base wage is set at the level corresponding to equilibrium in the absence of shocks. The indexing parameter is

$$\gamma = \frac{\log W - \log W^*}{\log P - \log P^*} \qquad (5.34)$$

where P^* is the base price level and W and P are the actual nominal wage and price levels. If γ is zero, price changes have no effect on wages and money wage is fixed. If γ is unity then the actual real wage (W/P) equals the base real wage (W^*/P^*) and the real wage is fixed. Once the contracts are agreed then the level of employment is demand determined.

The model being considered is (5.27), (5.28) and (5.33). Substituting from (5.28) into (5.27) gives

$$\log Y = \frac{-\delta}{1-\delta} (\log R - u) + \delta K + u \qquad (5.35)$$

and putting this in (5.33) reduces to

$$\log \bar{M} = k + \log W - \frac{1}{1-\delta} \log R + \frac{u}{1-\delta} + \delta K \qquad (5.36)$$

To see the effects of indexation when there are real shocks we first examine the non-indexed case. If u changes from zero to a positive number, then since the nominal wage W is fixed, from (5.36), the real wage R must increase above its previous value. From (5.28) this suggests that the demand for labour falls, but this ignores the effect of u. An increase in u increases output, from (5.27), at any given level of labour input, and so there is a productivity increase which exactly offsets the effects of the increase in the wage rate (see Gray (1976) pp. 228–9 for details). This can be observed from (5.36) since differentiating with respect to u gives

$$\frac{d \log R}{du} = 1$$

Consequently, from (5.28)

$$\frac{d \log L^d}{du} = 0$$

It follows from (5.27) that the change in output is equal to the size of the shock and the variance of output in the non-indexed case is

$$\sigma_{YNI}^2 = \sigma_u^2$$

which is the variance of the real shock.

For the fully indexed economy, the real wage rate is fixed at the initial value R^*. The increase in u in (5.28) increases the demand for labour and there is no offsetting effect from R. Thus L^D is higher and, from (5.27), output is higher both through the direct impact of a higher u and also through the indirect effect $(\delta/1 - \delta)$ because L is higher. The variance of output in this case is

$$\sigma_{YI}^2 = \left(\frac{1}{1-\delta}\right)^2 \sigma_u^2$$

Comparing the two cases the indexed variance is larger if

$$\left(\frac{1}{1-\delta}\right)^2 > 1$$

Since $\delta < 1$, this condition holds and hence indexation can exacerbate the effect of real shocks on output, relative to the non-indexed case. This is illustrated in Figure 5.1 where in quadrant (a) the relationship between the real wage and the real shock is shown in the two cases. In quadrant (b) the demand for labour is shown and quadrant (c) gives the production function. Prior to the shock ($u = 0$) the values of the variables are R_0, L_0 and Y_0. With full indexation the favourable shock $\bar{u}$ leaves the real wage at R_0, increases the demand for labour (by $1/1 - \delta$ from (5.28)) and employment increases to L_I. From (5.27) the production function shifts and, with higher employment, output is Y_I. With no indexation the real wage rises to R_{NI}, employment is unchanged but because of the shift in the production function output is higher than before the shock. We observe that

$$Y_I > Y_{NI} > Y_0, \quad L_I > L_{NI} = L_0, \quad R_{NI} > R_I = R_0$$

and so indexation increases the effects of a real shock on output.

We now consider the effects of a monetary shock on the Gray model.

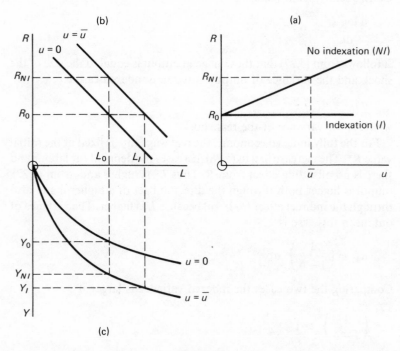

Figure 5.1

Equation (5.30) is replaced by

$$\log M^s = \log \bar{M} + v \tag{5.37}$$

where v is the monetary shock and if the model is solved as previously, (5.33) and 5.36) are modified by the extra term $-v$ on the right hand side. With no indexation, the effect of the nominal shock, since W is fixed, is to reduce real wages (from (5.36) modified) which results in a higher demand for labour and higher output. Thus a monetary shock effects real output. With full indexation, the nominal shock does not affect the real wage rate or the production function *per se* so that real output is unchanged. This is illustrated in Figure 5.2. Comparing the variables in the two cases we have

$$Y_{NI} > Y_I = Y_0, \quad R_{NI} < R_I = R_0, \quad L_{NI} > L_I = L_0$$

The effect of full indexation is to insulate the real sector of the economy from monetary shocks.

To summarise, a nominal shock affects real output if there is no indexation whereas there is no effect on real output with indexation.

The main conclusion to emerge from this examination of Gray's model is that whilst indexation insulates the real sector from the effects of monetary shocks it may exacerbate the real effects of real shocks.

However, this analysis uses the restrictive assumption that with indexation, employment is determined by the demand curve for labour.

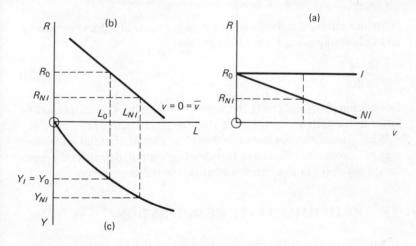

Figure 5.2

Cukierman (1980) points out that this assumption is arbitrary. Elementary demand and supply analysis would predict that if the real-wage rate is above the equilibrium real wage then employment will be demand determined.

Conversely, if the real wage is below the equilibrium level then employment will be fixed by the supply curve. Cukierman replaces Gray's assumption with one where employment is determined as a weighted average of the demand and supply quantities corresponding to the real wage. Hence, from (5.28) and (5.29),

$$\log L = a\left(-\frac{1}{1-\delta} \log R - u + K \right) + (1-a)(\phi \log R + K) \quad (5.38)$$

where a is a constant. If a is unity then (5.38) reduces to (5.28) and we have the Gray (or Fischer, 1977) model. Conversely, if a is zero, employment is determined by the supply curve and (5.38) reduces to (5.29). The new model is (5.27), (5.29) and (5.33). Substitution into (5.33) gives

$$\log \bar{M} = k + \log W - (1 - \delta\phi) \log R + \delta K + u \quad (5.39)$$

With no indexation, W is fixed and so a negative value of u (to keep employment determined on the supply curve) changes $\log R$ by $u/(1 - \delta\phi)$. From (5.29) and (5.27) we have the change in $\log Y$ is

$$\frac{d \log Y}{du} = \frac{1}{1 - \delta\phi} \quad (5.40)$$

With indexation, R is fixed and so a negative value of u does not effect L and only changes $\log Y$ via (5.27) so that

$$\frac{d \log Y}{du} = 1 \quad (5.41)$$

Comparing (5.40) and (5.41), the impact of a real shock on output will be lower in the fully indexed case if $(1 - \delta\phi)$ is less than one.

What Cukierman has shown is that Gray's result, that full indexation may exacerbate the effects of a real shock on output, depends very much on the assumption that employment is demand determined.

5.5 THE OPTIMAL LEVEL OF INDEXATION

In our discussion in the previous sections of this chapter we saw that while indexation may stabilise the economy in the case of nominal shocks it may make worse the effects of real shocks. This suggests that there may be some intermediate level of indexation, between zero and unity, which is optimal. In order to decide whether this is so a model must be specified which includes an appropriate welfare function. Gray adopts a loss function expressed in terms of output alone so that the optimal level of indexation is one which produces the smallest fluctuation of output in response to shocks. Full indexation occurs when there are no real shocks to the economy. Zero indexation occurs when there are no nominal shocks and the labour supply curve is perfectly inelastic in response to the real wage, i.e. ϕ is zero in (5.29). These results are now demonstrated more formally. The non-mathematical reader may prefer to move to (5.52) which gives the result.

The loss function adopted by Gray is

$$G = E(\log Y - \log Y_0)^2 \tag{5.42}$$

where Y_0 is the 'desired' or full information level and Y the actual level of output. The desired level of output is that level which occurs when labour supply (5.29) and labour demand (5.28) are equal, given full information on the shocks. Equating (5.28) and (5.29) results in

$$\log R = \frac{u}{\phi(1-\delta)+1} \tag{5.43}$$

and hence substituting (5.43) into (5.29) gives the equilibrium level of employment

$$\log L_0 = \frac{\phi u}{\phi(1-\delta)+1} + K \tag{5.44}$$

so that from (5.27)

$$\log Y_0 = \frac{\delta\phi u}{\phi(1-\delta)+1} + \delta K + u \tag{5.45}$$

Next, the actual level of output is required. Reverting to the assumption that employment is demand-determined, substitution from (5.28) into (5.27) gives

$$\log Y = \frac{-\delta}{1-\delta}(\log R - u) + \delta K + u \tag{5.46}$$

Gray (1976, Appendix 1) shows that the solution of the model for $\log R$ is

$$\log R = (\gamma - 1)(v - \log Y + \delta K) \tag{5.47}$$

where γ is the indexation parameter and hence that

$$\log Y = \frac{1}{1 - \delta\gamma}[v\delta(1-\gamma) + u + \delta K(1 - \delta\gamma)] \tag{5.48}$$

By subtraction of (5.45) from (5.48)

$$\log Y - \log Y_0 = \frac{\delta}{1 - \delta\gamma}\{v(1-\gamma) + uF\} \tag{5.49}$$

where $F = \dfrac{\gamma\phi + \gamma - \phi}{1 + \phi(1 - \delta)}$ $\qquad\qquad$ (5.50)

and hence, by substitution into (5.42)

$$G = \frac{\delta^2}{(1 - \delta\gamma)^2}(\sigma_v^2(1-\gamma)^2 + \sigma_u^2 F^2) \tag{5.51}$$

where σ_v^2 and σ_u^2 are the variances of v and u respectively. To maximise welfare, the loss function is minimised and the first-order conditions for a minimum are obtained by setting the derivative with respect to γ to zero. After some tedious algebra, the optimal degree of indexation is

$$\gamma = \frac{\sigma_u^2\phi + \sigma_v^2(1-\delta)(1 + \phi(1-\delta))}{\sigma_u^2(1+\phi) + \sigma_v^2(1-\delta)(1 + \phi(1-\delta))} \tag{5.52}$$

Because ϕ is positive it is clear on inspection that this is between zero and one. If there are no real shocks in the economy ($\sigma_u^2 = 0$) then the optimal degree of indexation is one, while if there are no nominal shocks ($\sigma_v^2 = 0$) then

$$\gamma = \frac{\phi}{1 + \phi} \tag{5.53}$$

The interpretation of this is that when real shocks occur optimal indexation reduces their impact on output.

Gray also notes that for an economy subject to both real and monetary shocks, increased monetary variability imposes costs on the system. This can be seen by differentiating (5.51) with respect to σ_v^2 to give

$$\frac{\partial G}{\partial \sigma_v^2} = \frac{\delta^2(1-\gamma)^2}{(1 - \delta\gamma)^2} \tag{5.54}$$

which will be positive if γ is not unity. That is, costs will be higher if σ_v^2 rises.

The results presented by Gray have been extended and modified by a number of researchers. Danziger (1981), for example, demonstrates that the optimal degree of indexation is not necessarily restricted to the range between zero and one if the shocks enter in a non-multiplicative manner. Pazner (1981) suggests an indexation scheme which includes full indexation to the price level and partial indexation to the level of income. This will insulate the real sector of the model from monetary shocks and reduce, though not eliminate, the impact of real shocks.

Karni (1983) points out that the 'optimal' indexation scheme considered by Gray aims to adjust wages to promote stability of output by relating indexation solely to changes in the price level. However, if the exact size of shocks which occur during the contract period can be determined *ex post* then Karni shows that, in general, optimal indexation schemes exist which dominate Gray's formulation. For example, Gray's indexation scheme (5.34) can be written as

$$\log(W/P) = (\gamma - 1)(\log P - \log P^*) \tag{5.55}$$

if $\log W^* - \log P^*$ is set to zero,
and this can be modified to allow for the impact of changes in the labour market on wages by putting

$$\log(W/P) = (\gamma - 1)(\log P - \log P^*) + b(\log Y - \log Y^*) \tag{5.56}$$

where b is a constant. From (5.45), $\log Y^*$ is equal to δK when u is zero. If the loss function proposed in the Gray model is minimised the new optimal value of γ equals 1 and b is equal to $1/(1 + \phi)$. This optimal indexation scheme eliminates totally the loss of welfare associated with fixing wages prior to observing the stochastic shocks. Notice further that Gray's assumption that employment is demand-determined does not matter here since supply and demand are equal at the optimum.

In general, the optimal form of indexation will depend upon the precise structure of the economy under consideration and will incorporate knowledge of all the variables which contain information relevant to the determination of the equilibrium wage rate. Karni's important point is that if all the shocks can be completely observed then optimal indexation schemes exist which can eliminate the welfare loss associated with the labour market conventions and replicate the auction outcome. In most cases wage indexation schemes do not alter the information structure of the economy. An exception to this occurs when a government introduces index-linked debt which might be interpreted by agents as a signal of an intention to reduce monetary expansion. That is, it adds credibility to an announced policy change. For this to be so there must be an asymmetry of information between public and private agents. With this exception, indexation schemes cannot replicate the full-information outcome if this is not the auction outcome. In the Gray model agents have full knowledge of the current state of the economy and are able to identify the source and magnitude of the different random shocks. These particular circumstances result in the auction outcome being the same as the full information outcome. If the assumption of full information is relaxed, however, the auction outcome will reflect this lack of information and will differ from the full information outcome.

What Karni has demonstrated is that optimal indexation schemes exist which in principle can replicate the auction outcome. This is feasible when the number of independent variables in the indexation formula equals the number of sources of noise relevant to the determination of the market clearing wage. More recently, the sensitivity of such optimal schemes to the nature of the exchange rate regime, the degree of openness of the economy and the type of monetary rules in operation have been analysed by Flood and Marion (1982), Aizenman and Frenkel (1985), Aizenman (1985), Bhandari (1982) and Turnovsky (1983). A number of these authors point out that the appropriate degree of wage indexation, the type of exchange rate intervention or what constitutes optimal monetary policy are not independent of each other. Current research is seeking a framework within which the choice of each of these is made by a joint optimization of public and private agents' utilities.

A further issue concerns the structural equations of the models from which optimal indexation schemes are derived. It may be unreasonable to assume that these equations are invariant to the postulated schemes. For example, with Karni's model, if firms re-optimise subject to the optimal indexation scheme, a different demand for labour schedule is obtained. This point may invalidate Karni's general conclusion that optimal indexation schemes can replicate the auction outcome. Further research is needed on this.

5.6 PRACTICAL CONSIDERATIONS

In this section we consider two issues. First, we examine why, in practice, indexation agreements link wages to prices alone. Secondly, we question why fixed-period wage contracts exist since in their absence there would appear to be no role for indexation if expectations are formed according to the rational expectations hypothesis.

Indexation agreements generally link wages solely to prices. As we saw in the previous section Karni (1983) points out that for an indexation scheme to be optimal it must be based on all the known independent variables in the economy, rather than just the price level. Nevertheless, one feature of the labour market is that contracts are rarely contingent on variables other than the price level. This implies that contracts freely agreed between workers and management involve a degree of inefficiency since nominal disturbances will normally have an impact on real variables. The demand for labour will not equal the supply so that the marginal product of labour (from the demand curve) and the marginal value of leisure (from the supply curve) will differ. There is an unexploited opportunity for mutual gains from trade. The crucial issue is why the parties would agree, *ex ante* to a form of wage contract which imposes this sort of *ex post* deadweight loss (see Barro, 1977).

One obvious explanation is that the 'fully contingent indexed wage contract' may be costly to write or enforce. That is, there are costs in contracting. Also, variables such as workers' productivity, which might appear in the 'optimal' contract, may be subject to the problem of moral hazard. Thus, if one variable within a contract depends upon the behaviour of a second variable which can be influenced by one of the parties, there will be an incentive to change this second variable in the appropriate direction (see Calvo and Phelps, 1977). Therefore there may be a trade-off between the 'optimal' contract, which preserves efficiency but is difficult to enforce, and non-contingent contracts which involve inefficiencies. Blanchard (1979) demonstrates that simple rules (such as the indexation of wages to the price level only) may be an optimal compromise in certain circumstances.

Turning to the second issue, we now consider why agents enter into contracts rather than engage in auction markets. In the Gray model both firms and workers are assumed to be risk neutral and the full-information outcome is also the auction outcome. Consequently it is not clear why agents would wish to negotiate fixed contracts. One rationale is that the auction outcome imposes costs which are higher than those incurred in writing (possibly contingent) contracts (see Gray, 1978). Alternatively, Azariadis (1975, 1978) shows that if workers are risk averse then the auction market for labour will not in general allocate risks efficiently between the parties. This is because an auction economy implies uncertain labour income and risk-averse employees may wish to negotiate a contract that protects labour income to some degree from fluctuations in demand and supply. With contracts, part of the risk of an uncertain labour demand is shifted to the firm which guarantees employees' wage rates. From this viewpoint, indexation agreements are institutional insurance policies against unexpected and generally uninsurable cyclical risks (see Azariadis, 1978) and the demand for escalator clauses will depend partly on the workers' ability to hedge against cyclical factors in the absence of such clauses. Gordon (1974) and Hall and Lilien (1979) also discuss the role of contracts.

Blinder (1977) and Shavell (1976) present models under which indexed financial assets will provide a substitute for escalator clauses. However, since workers mostly derive their incomes from wages, even if capital markets are perfect and workers are able to acquire index-linked bonds, the use of human capital as their ultimate collateral limits the size of these bonds.

5.7 CONCLUSIONS

In this chapter we have examined the role of indexation or escalator clauses in the labour market. Viewed as a form of incomes policy they have the advantage of allowing variation in the wage rates negotiated in different sectors of the economy. If it is assumed that agents form their expectations in an adaptive manner then indexation can insulate the real economy from monetary changes. This can provide the rationale for a government committed to a policy of monetary contraction for introducing compulsory escalator clauses in wage contracts in order to remove the real dislocations that would otherwise occur.

In contrast, if it is assumed that agents' expectations are formed rationally then we saw in section 5.3 that it is possible for indexation to exacerbate the effects of real shocks on the level of output. This was confirmed in section 5.4 when Gray's Model was discussed and both real and nominal shocks were considered. The results imply that there may be a trade-off of the effects of real shocks against the effects of nominal shocks. The possibility of an optimal degree of indexation existing which differs from full indexation and no indexation, was examined in section 5.5.

Finally in section 5.6 we reviewed why indexation is generally to a subset of available information, namely prices and why contracts occur. We saw agents enter contracts for reasons of risk sharing or costs of negotiations.

6 The Future of Wage and Price Controls

6.1 INTRODUCTION

The case for some form of prices and incomes policy can be made out on two quite separate grounds. The first depends on the belief that inflation is caused by cost–push factors. In this case a prices and incomes policy is directed towards the root cause of inflation and would achieve its aims by inducing moderation of wage claims. Clearly it would normally be necessary for the policy to be accompanied by some palliatives to secure trade union agreement for implementation of the policy. As indicated in Chapters 2 and 5, it is our belief that pure cost–push models have little empirical validity so that we do not pursue this argument any further.

The second reason often given for the introduction of a prices and incomes policy is based on the high costs associated with stagflation. For example both Layard (1982) and Meade (1985) explicitly argue that unemployment has to be maintained at quite high levels to prevent accelerating inflation. Reduction of unemployment by demand management policies would, in their view, lead to an increase in the rate of inflation. Consequently the role of a prices and incomes policy is to secure a lower level of unemployment. Furthermore both Meade and Layard advocate the use of differing types of incomes policies over quite long time horizons. This stance is clearly illustrated by referring to the simple macroeconomic model presented in Chapter 5 (5.1) to (5.4) when expectations are formed adaptively. Subsequent solution of the model for p and y in (5.5) and (5.6) demonstrate the two-fold proposition (i) decreasing the rate of monetary growth reduces both inflation and output with the fall in output occurring prior to that in expectations and (ii) adjustment towards the new equilibrium is slow. This analysis begs two questions. First, in practice, how slow is the adjustment described above? Secondly, would a prices and incomes policy help to improve the situation?

In Chapter 2 we examined the empirical evidence concerning the type of prices and incomes policy commonly introduced in a number of countries over the last twenty years. This evidence is flawed since there is no allowance for the effects of an anticipation of future wage and price

123

controls. *A priori* it seems reasonable to assume that economic agents will take account of expected controls. For example, if it is believed that a wage freeze is likely to be introduced in six months time then, *ceteris paribus*, the length of wage contracts and frequency of wage settlements are likely to change during the next six months. It follows, therefore, that the transition path of inflation, wage settlements and hence real quantities are likely to depend on the actual or anticipated implementation of wage and price controls. Formal allowance for this point in empirical work may well change the estimated impact of controls. In theory, a largely unanticipated incomes policy could have favourable implications for the transition path of economic variables towards their equilibrium values. This might be particularly true where the credibility of the government is low so that a contractionary monetary policy on its own is likely to have its main impact on output and employment rather than on nominal variables.

We also discussed some of the microeconomic effects of prices and incomes policies. There seems to be strong theoretical support for the view that wage and price controls may impose a dead-weight loss on the economy by distorting relative prices. No attempt has been made to quantify this loss. However, the overall cost/benefit analysis assessment of conventional incomes policies must weigh these microeconomic costs against any benefits which arise from the macroeconomic effects.

From our review of the literature on tax-based incomes policies (TIP) in Chapter 3, it is clear that such policies can affect the demand for labour and reduce the equilibrium unemployment rate. *A priori* the major disadvantages of such a scheme concern the possible distortions it causes. First there is the impact of the administration of the scheme. Secondly, and perhaps more important, firms are likely to change the structure of their labour force and implicit wage payments (i.e. fringe benefits) in response to the tax incentives associated with the use of a single wage norm for all grades of labour. TIPs appear at first sight to distort the labour market to a lesser degree than conventional incomes policies since they permit some flexibility in wage payments albeit at some potential cost in the form of extra tax payments. However the issue is not so clear cut. Any cost/benefit analysis must allow for the distortions caused both by the implementation of a TIP *per se* as well as those due to the differing impact of real and nominal shocks. For example, if shocks are predominantly nominal, then relative prices may be distorted to a lesser degree by a wage freeze than by a TIP. Of course the macroeconomic implications of a TIP on the rate of inflation in the short run are potentially radically different from those of a conventional policy. Consequently the cost/benefit choice between a TIP and a conventional policy is not clear cut and could well depend on the particular circumstances prevailing in the economy.

In Chapter 4, we examined the general nature and implications of final offer arbitration (FOA). Apart from the Meade proposal, FOA is not a policy which can be regarded as concerned with inflation *per se*. Since, as we noted in Chapter 4, the last offers of both parties could exceed the arbitrator's preferred figure, FOA appears to be an inefficient way of controlling wages and prices. Indeed, FOA was not devised as a method of imposing a settlement on firms or unions but rather as a means of providing an incentive for risk averse parties to agree settlements without involving strikes or lockouts. In our view, FOA could have a potential role in areas where strikes are deemed to be inconsistent with the general public interest. However, for the use of FOA not to be prejudicial to the interests of either party, it may be necessary to offer some inducements to secure its successful implementation.

Indexation schemes were discussed in Chapter 5. We showed that in an economy where expectations adjust slowly to changed monetary conditions indexation could help to insulate real variables from monetary changes. However, if expectations are formed rationally, efficient indexation of wages to prices alone will imply that the relevant coefficient is less than unity when the economy is subject to real shocks. Moreover, in these circumstances, full indexation to the price level alone may exacerbate the impact of real shocks in the economy. Recent findings suggest that an optimal indexation scheme would index wages to all endogenous variables which convey independent information about shocks within the economy. The difficulty of implementing such a scheme is that problems of moral hazard could make the relevant contracts costly to write and enforce even if the parties had the type of information postulated in the formal models. This may explain why wage contracts are apparently only rarely fully contingent on the price level in the absence of government incomes policies.

Consequently compulsory indexation will provide most benefits where shocks are mainly monetary in origin and expectations are slow to adjust. In these circumstances indexation to the price level will minimise the impact of monetary changes on real variables and as a result the link between monetary change and inflation is speeded up. It is, of course, precisely this feature that may make compulsory indexation unattractive to governments which pursue inflationary macroeconomic policies. Furthermore, if private agents are presumed to possess as much information as the government, then compulsory indexation schemes would appear to be virtually irrelevant. Private agents can renegotiate their own 'optimal' schemes which would offset the government imposed scheme. If the compulsory scheme also legislates against private arrangements then a conventional incomes policy can be interpreted as a special case of indexation. For example if the indexation scheme is defined by:

$$w = a + bp \tag{6.1}$$

where a and b are constants and w and p are changes in wages and prices respectively, then when $b = 0$, equation (6.1) defines a conventional incomes policy with the 'norm' equalling a.

On reflection there is an additional feature of optimal compulsory schemes that private agents acting freely in a largely unregulated labour market may not be able to replicate or improve upon. The optimal actions of any one union or firm will typically depend on the actions of other unions or firms. A compulsory policy may help to solve this coordination problem more easily than by leaving private agents to their own devices (see for example Maital and Benjamini, 1980). It is from this perspective that we consider the novel proposal recently advanced by Weitzman (1983) and (1984). His idea can be interpreted as a form of indexation scheme with wages indexed to the performance of the employing firm. This may help to solve the coordination problem raised above. Weitzman takes a rather pessimistic view of the consequences of stagflation. He also feels that the elimination of inflation would require unacceptably high levels of unemployment for quite long periods of time. In reviewing the various alternatives to 'tight money' such as 'do nothing', 'wage price controls' and 'tax based incomes policies', his pessimistic conclusion is that 'there are no obvious solutions' (Weitzman, 1984, p. 71). His view is that the wage system must be radically changed and in the next section we examine his ideas.

6.2   A SHARE ECONOMY

Weitzman's suggestion is for a 'share economy' in which the reward for labour is related to the performance of the firm. As an introduction and in order to demonstrate the general nature of his arguments, we use the simple example provided by Weitzman (1984) pp. 4–6 and (1983) p. 764. Suppose that the wages (including fringe benefits) of the employees of the General Motors Corporation (GMC) come to $24 per hour. Assuming profit maximisation implies that the marginal revenue product (mrp) of labour is also $24 per hour. The average revenue product (arp) is, of course higher, to cover overheads, profits, etc., say $36 per hour. Suppose now that the wage contract is replaced by a share contract, that is, rather than being paid a wage workers receive a proportion of the firm's revenue. The total revenue of GMC is divided into two parts: two thirds to the work force and one third to management. If 500 000 workers are employed total revenue will be $18 million per hour of which $12 m goes to the work force and $6 m to management. At first sight, nothing seems to have changed. This is not so if we consider the situation from the point of view of the firm. Abstracting from the fact that increased sales by GMC would require a reduction in price because of the downward sloping demand curve, if an extra worker is employed the net revenue of GMC increases by $8 per hour. This turns the firm into an active seeker of workers in the same way that a firm, under conditions of imperfect competition, is an active seeker of markets at the current price which exceeds marginal cost. To illustrate this point further, note that when an extra worker is employed the increase in total revenue is $24 (i.e. the mrp of labour) but total earnings of labour are now $12 000 016 (i.e. $\frac{2}{3} \times$ $18 000 024). The net revenue for GMC is $8 000 008. The gain of $8 for GMC is matched by a decline in the hourly pay for each worker from $24 to $23.99998 (i.e. 12 000 016/500 001). If all firms operate under a share contract, each firm will actively seek workers with equilibrium in the labour market being established where 'all qualified persons in an economy seeking work have a job' (Weitzman, 1984, p. 6). The analysis now proceeds more formally.

Currently a wage compensation system is the standard form of rewarding labour. The major portion of a worker's earnings come from the fixed or quasi contractual wage which is subject to negotiation at fixed intervals, normally annually in the UK. Additional remuneration may take the form of overtime payments and bonus payments but the central thesis remains that the basic wage is only loosely tied to the firm's performance. A wage compensation system may be described by:

$$W_i = F_i(Q_i;Z_i) \tag{6.2}$$

where W_i = wage paid by the ith firm

Q_i = slow moving contract parameter

Z_i = fast moving current performance indicator (e.g output or revenue)

The traditional wage compensation system can be written as:

$$F(Q_i;Z_i) = Q_i \tag{6.3}$$

with $\partial F_i / \partial Z_i > 0$ (6.4)

The profit maximising firm will employ labour up to the point where its marginal revenue product (mrp) equals the marginal cost of labour. As far as the product market is concerned, the vast majority of firms employing labour will face a downward sloping demand curve for their products so that:

$$MR = P(1 - 1/e)$$ (6.5)

where e = price elasticity of demand for the product.
Rearranging (6.5) produces:

$$P = [e/(e-1)]MR$$ (6.6)

where the item in the square brackets represents what Weitzman calls the mark-up coefficient. This coefficient will of course vary between firms so that firms facing a relative elastic demand for their products will have a mark-up coefficient approaching unity. Standard microeconomic theory suggests that the three decisions made by a profit maximising firm will be:

(a) Output is set at the level where marginal revenue equals marginal cost.
(b) A sufficient quantity of labour to produce that output is hired by the firm.
(c) The price is determined by multiplying marginal cost by the mark-up coefficient.

Using (a) and (c) above, the price charged by the firm will be:

$$P = [e/(e-1)]MC$$ (6.7)

The crucial point about the wage contract is how employment and wage levels react to a shock to the economy. Given the existence of wage contracts which prevent money wages from falling in the short run, the response of individual earnings to a decline in the performance of the firm is likely to be quite small. Consequently we may define a wage compensation system as one that approximates the condition:

$$\partial W_i / \partial L_i = 0$$ (6.8)

where L_i is the labour input of the ith firm.

We now examine how employment is affected by a contractionary shock. Clearly the firm cannot sell as much as before at the same price and the vital question is whether quantities or prices are reduced.

Weitzman argues that it is a reasonable approximation to the truth to assume that demand has been reduced uniformly at each price and that, therefore, the price elasticity of demand for the product and the mark-up coefficient will remain approximately the same. He further argues that, given constant money wages, marginal cost will also remain roughly constant in the production range. These assumptions imply little change in the prices charged by firms so that the typical response of an individual firm to a fall off in demand is to cut back production and lay off workers.

A firm faces two kinds of uncertainty and shocks to its wellbeing. The first is firm specific so that firm *A* experiences a shock which reduces demand for its products whilst other firms in the economy will be experiencing increased demand for their products. In these circumstances the price mechanism will work well to co-ordinate the economy. Labour released by firm *A* will be absorbed by these other firms. This contrasts with the position of the other type of uncertainty which concerns the general state of aggregate demand. In this case, the analysis described above predicts that most, if not all, firms will be laying off labour. There is little offsetting increase in demand elsewhere so that total unemployment rises. Weitzman (1984) concludes that 'the current wage system of compensating labour is a perilous anachronism that needs to be replaced' (p. 46).

His view is that the appropriate replacement for the wage compensation system is a *share contract*, that is a system of reward to labour which links the wage of the employee to a firm specific indicator such as, for example, revenue or profit. As was pointed out in the illustrative example the remuneration per worker declines as more workers are employed so that a share contract may be defined as one where:

$$\partial W_i / \partial L_i < 0 \tag{6.9}$$

Reverting back to the simple example at the beginning of this section, it will be recalled that the addition of an extra worker added more to revenue than cost so that each company has an incentive to employ extra labour. As the firm increases production so the prices of its products will fall because the individual firm normally faces a downward-sloping demand curve. However, if all firms are keen to expand production, the increased spending by all workers will tend to increase demand for products in general.

The next important question posed is what happens to employment during a general recession. The share firm will react by trying to retain workers and lower prices. Workers' earnings will fall but employment will hold up. Only if wages in a particular industry or firm fall below the general level of earnings for similar types of workers, will workers leave that industry. Consequently in a general recession there is an automatic equilibrating system which Weitzman claims cannot be replicated by making wages more flexible. In the case of perfect wage flexibility equilibrium is continuously maintained. In the case of a share economy shocks are still occurring but the response to the shock is directed to reducing prices rather than quantities. The final general point about the scheme concerns the choice of the indicator to measure the firm's performance. As noted earlier this could either be total revenue earned by the firm or alternatively profits. The selection of the indicator seems to be a matter of little importance compared with the general principle but it should be noted that use of profits would entail a minimum wage level being fixed since the level of profits for a firm can be negative.

If a share economy provides an incentive to the reduction in unemployment the question naturally arises whether it provides a corresponding stimulus to inflation. Weitzman argues that this is not the case because, in a share economy, the absorption of extra labour arises from the supply rather than demand side. Expansion of output requires firms to lower prices as they move down their demand curve. A contrast is made between the response of the two economies to a supply side shock such as an increase in oil prices. The wage compensation firm will respond by raising prices and laying-off workers. In the share economy the adjustment would be attained without necessarily raising all prices or causing unemployment but of course real earnings of labour would fall.

The nub of the proposal is the replacement of the relative security of wage rates under a wage compensation system by relative security of employment under a share system. Whether the change would be acceptable to the labour force is a moot point. It is apparently the case that employees prefer contracts which guarantee pay rates rather than employment levels. A second difficulty arises concerning the relative shares which accrue to labour and management respectively (i.e. two thirds and one third respectively in the example at the beginning of this section). This is, to say the least, a likely source of much dispute. As an inducement to accepting the system, Weitzman suggests that tax concessions may be given on all income received as a genuine share contract such as, for example, profit sharing schemes etc. Also to ease the administrative burden it is suggested that introduction of the scheme should be restricted to companies whose shares are quoted on the stock exchange. Apart from administrative convenience, this would have the added advantage of concentrating on employees whose earnings vary least with the value of output. Included in the smaller firms are the self-employed, partnerships, etc., where earnings are strongly linked to the performance of their firms. Thirdly, there is the problem of public sector employees. For the vast majority, there is no associated revenue which can be apportioned. It hardly seems conducive to good industrial relations for the economy to be divided into two sectors. For the private sector earnings will be adjusted automatically according to the performance of the employing firms. In contrast, public sector employees will benefit from security of both employment and wage rates. Finally a compromise may be possible by the use of tax incentives to promote greater use of profit-sharing schemes or, for that matter, co-ownership of firms by way of share distribution to employees. This may help to solve the problems of stagflation without undertaking a radical reform on the lines advocated by Weitzman. Such schemes would be best directed towards employees of individual firms rather than the labour force in general.

6.3 CONCLUSIONS

We have surveyed a number of variations of incomes policies and also a suggestion involving a radical reform of the labour compensation system. Our conclusions regarding the efficacy of such schemes tend towards pessimism rather than optimism. Nevertheless we feel that they may provide some influences which tend to moderate the growth of unemployment whilst other anti-inflationary policies are being pursued. In particular it is difficult to believe *a priori* that the potential costs associated with the introduction of a share scheme or indeed a TIP into an already highly distorted labour market can be regarded as being excessive in relation to the potential benefits accruing from reduced unemployment.

References

ADAM, J. (ed.) (1982) *Employment Policies in the Soviet Union and Eastern Europe* (London: Macmillan).

ADDISON, J. T. (1979) *Wage Policies and Collective Bargaining Developments in Finland, Ireland and Norway* (Paris: OECD).

ADDISON, J. T. (1981) 'Incomes policy: the recent European experience' in Fallick and Elliott (1981).

AIZENMAN, J. (1985) 'Wage flexibility and openness', *Quarterly Journal of Economics*, vol. 100, pp. 539–50.

AIZENMAN, J. and FRENKEL, J. A. (1985) 'Optimal wage indexation, foreign exchange intervention and monetary policy', *American Economic Review*, vol. 75, pp. 402–23.

ALBEDA, W. (1985) 'Recent trends in collective bargaining in the Netherlands', *International Labour Review*, vol. 124, pp. 49–60.

ARTIS, M. (1981) 'Incomes policies: some rationales' in Fallick and Elliott (1981).

ASHENFELTER, O. C. and PENCAVEL, J. H. (1975) 'Wage changes and the frequency of wage settlements', *Economica*, vol. 42, pp. 162–70.

AZARIADIS, C. (1975) 'Implicit contracts and underemployment equilibria', *Journal of Political Economy*, vol. 83, pp. 1183–202.

AZARIADIS, C. (1978) 'Escalator clauses and the allocation of cyclical risks', *Journal of Economic Theory*, vol. 18, pp. 119–55.

BARRO, R. J. (1977) 'Long-term contracting, sticky prices and monetary policy', *Journal of Monetary Economics*, vol. 3, pp. 305–16.

BAUMOL, W. J. (1959) *Economic Dynamics* (London: Macmillan).

BEETON, D. J. (1985) 'Contingent wage agreements: the historical and international evidence on their determinants and effects', *Department of Economics Paper*, no. 140, Queen Mary College, University of London.

BHANDARI, J. S. (1982) 'Staggered wage setting and exchange rate policy in an economy with capital assets', *Journal of International Money and Finance*, vol. 1, pp. 275–92.

BLACK, S. W. and KELEJIAN, H. H. (1970) 'A macro model of the U.S. labor market', *Econometrica*, vol. 38, pp. 712–41.

BLANCHARD, O. J. (1979) 'Wage indexing rules and the behaviour of the economy', *Journal of Political Economy*, vol. 87, pp. 798–815.

BLINDER, A. S. (1977) 'Indexing the economy through financial intermediation' in Brunner and Meltzer (1977).

BLINDER, A. S. and NEWTON, W. J. (1981) 'The 1971–1974 controls program and the price level', *Journal of Monetary Economics*, vol. 8, pp. 1–23.

BOSANQUET, N. (1983) 'Tax-based incomes policies', pp. 33–49 in Robinson and Mayhew (1983).

BOSTON, J. (1984) *Incomes Policy in New Zealand* (Wellington: Victoria University Press).

BOX, G. E. P. and JENKINS, G. M. (1970) *Time-Series Analysis: Forecasting and Control* (San Francisco: Holden-Day).

BOX, G. E. P. and TIAO, G. C. (1975) 'Intervention analysis with applications to economic and environmental problems', *Journal of the American Statistical Association*, vol. 70, pp. 70–9.

BRITTAN, S. and LILLEY, P. (1977) *The Delusion of Incomes Policy* (London: Temple Smith).

BRUNNER, K. and MELTZER, A. H. (eds) (1976) *The Economics of Price and Wage Controls*, Carnegie-Rochester Conference Series on Public Policy, vol. 2 (Amsterdam: North-Holland).

BRUNNER, K. and MELTZER, A. H. (eds) (1977) *Stabilization of the Domestic and International Economy*, Carnegie-Rochester Conference Series on Public Policy, vol. 5 (Amsterdam: North-Holland).

BURROWS, P. and HITIRIS, T. (1972) 'Estimating the impact of incomes policy', *Bulletin of Economic Research*, vol. 24, pp. 42–51.

CALVO, G. A. and PHELPS, E. S. (1977) 'Employment contingent wage contracts' in Brunner and Meltzer (1977).

CAVES, R. E. and KRAUSE, L. B. (eds) (1984) *The Australian Economy: a View from the North* (Sydney: George Allen and Unwin).

CHAPMAN, D. R. and JUNOR, C. W. (1981) 'Profits, variability of profits and the Price Justification Tribunal', *Economic Record*, vol. 57, pp. 128–39.

CHRISTOFIDES, L. N. (1985) 'The impact of controls on wage contract duration', *The Economic Journal*, vol. 95, pp. 161–8.

COHEN, R. (1974) *Labour and Politics in Nigeria 1945–71* (London: Heinemann).

Congressional Budget Office (1977) *Incomes Policies in the United States: Historical Review and some Issues* (Washington D. C.: The Congress of the United States).

COX, C. C. (1980) 'The enforcement of public price controls', *Journal of Political Economy*, vol. 88, pp. 887–916.

CUCKIERMAN, A. (1980) 'The effects of wage indexation on macroeconomic fluctuations: a generalisation', *Journal of Monetary Economics*, vol. 6, pp. 147–70.

DABSCHECK, B. (1975) 'The 1975 national wage case: now we have an incomes policy', *Journal of Industrial Relations*, vol. 17, pp. 298–309.

DABSCHECK, B. (1977) 'The PJT: a perverse case of window dressing', *Journal of Industrial Relations*, vol. 19, pp. 133–45.

DABSCHECK, B. (1978) 'National wage case decisions in 1977: the full bench survives but yet another year', *Journal of Industrial Relations*, vol. 20, pp. 67–71.

DANZIGER, L. (1981) 'On optimal wage indexation when shocks are real', *Economics Letters*, vol. 7, pp. 51–3.

DARBY, M. R. (1976) 'Price and wage controls: the first two years', in Brunner and Meltzer (1976).

DEAN, A. (1981) 'Incomes policy and the British economy in the 1970s' in R. E. J. Chater, A. Dean and R. F. Elliott (eds) *Incomes Policy* (Oxford: Clarendon Press).

DESAI, M., KEIL, M. and WADHWANI, S. (1984) 'Incomes policy in a political environment: a structural model for the UK 1961–80' in A. Hughes-Hallett (ed.) *Applied Decision Analysis and Economic Behaviour* (The Hague: Kluwer and Nijhoff).

134 *References*

DILDINE, L. L. and SUNLEY, E. M. (1978) 'Administrative problems of tax-based incomes policies', in Okun and Perry (1978).

DOLTON, P. J. and TREBLE, J. G. (1985) 'On final offer and not quite compulsory arbitration', *Scottish Journal of Political Economy*, vol. 32, pp. 181–90.

DONN, C. B. (1977) 'Games final-offer arbitrators might play', *Industrial Relations*, vol. 16, pp. 306–14.

ECKSTEIN, O. and BRINNER, R. (1972) 'The inflation process in the United States', *Joint Economic Committee*, 72–1710, pp. 1–46.

EDGREN, G., FAXEN, K. -O. and ODHNER, C. -E. (1973) *Wage Formation and the Economy* (London: George Allen and Unwin).

FALLICK, J. L. and ELLIOTT, R. F. (eds) (1981) *Incomes Policies, Inflation and Relative Pay* (London: George Allen and Unwin).

FARBER, H. S. (1981) 'Splitting the difference in interest arbitration', *Industrial and Labor Relations Review*, vol. 35, pp. 70–7.

FARBER, H. S. and KATZ, H. C. (1979) 'Interest arbitration, outcomes and the incentive to bargain', *Industrial and Labor Relations Review*, vol. 33, pp. 55–63.

FEIGE, E. L. and PEARCE, D. K. (1976) 'Inflation and incomes policy: an application of time series models', in Brunner and Meltzer (1976).

FELS, A. (1981) 'Policies for prices' in K. Hancock (ed.) *Incomes Policy in Australia* (Sydney: Harcourt Brace Jovanovich).

FEUILLE, P. (1979) 'Selected benefits and costs of compulsory arbitration', *Industrial and Labor Relations Review*, vol. 33, pp. 64–76.

FISCHER, S. (1977) 'Wage indexation and macroeconomic stability', in Brunner and Meltzer (1977).

FISHBEIN, W. H. (1984) *Wage Restraint By Consensus* (London: Routledge and Kegan Paul).

FLANAGAN, R. J., SOSKICE, D. W. and ULMAN, L. (1983) *Unionism, Economic Stabilization and Incomes Policies: European Experience* (Washington D. C.: The Brookings Institution).

FLOOD, R. P. and MARION, N. P. (1982) 'The transmission of disturbances under alternative exchange rate regimes with optimal indexation', *Quarterly Journal of Economics*, vol. 97, pp. 43–66.

FONSECA, A. J. (1975) *Wage Issues in a Developing Economy* (Bombay: Oxford University Press).

FRIEDMAN, M. (1968) 'The role of monetary policy', *American Economic Review*, vol. 58, pp. 1–17.

FRIEDMAN, M. (1974) 'Monetary corrections: a proposal for escalator clauses to reduce the costs of ending inflation', *Institute of Economic Affairs Occasional Paper*, no. 41.

GODFREY, L. (1971) 'The Phillips curve: incomes policy and trade union effects' in Johnson and Nobay (1971).

GOODWIN, C. D. (ed.) (1975) *Exhortation and Controls: The Search for a Wage-Price Policy 1945–71* (Washington D. C.: The Brookings Institution).

GORDON, D. F. (1974) 'A neo-classical theory of Keynesian unemployment', *Economic Inquiry*, vol. 12, pp. 431–59.

GORDON, R. J. (1970) 'The recent acceleration of inflation and its lessons for the future', *Brookings Papers on Economic Activity*, pp. 8–41.

GRAVELLE, H. and REES, R. (1981) *Microeconomics* (London: Longman).
GRAY, J. A. (1976) 'Wage indexation: a macroeconomic approach', *Journal of Monetary Economics*, vol. 2, pp. 221–35.
GRAY, J. A. (1978) 'On indexation and contract length', *Journal of Political Economy*, vol. 86, pp. 1–18.
HALL, R. E. and LILIEN, D. A. (1979) 'Efficient wage bargains under uncertain supply and demand', *American Economic Review*, vol. 69, pp. 868–79.
HARRIS, J. R. and TODARO, M. R. (1970) 'Migration, unemployment and development: a two sector analysis', *American Economic Review*, vol. 60, pp. 126–42.
HENRY, S. G. B. (1981) 'Incomes policy and aggregate pay' in Fallick and Elliott (1981).
HENRY, S. G. B. and ORMEROD, P. (1978) 'Incomes policy and wage inflation: empirical evidence for the UK 1961–1977', *National Institute Economic Review*, vol. 85, pp. 31–9.
HENRY, S. G. B., SAWYER, M. C. and SMITH, P. (1976) 'Models of inflation in the United Kingdom: an evaluation', *National Institute Economic Review*, no. 77, pp. 60–71.
HEY, J. D. (1979) *Uncertainty in Microeconomics* (Oxford: Martin Robertson).
HICKS, J. R. (1963) *The Theory of Wages* (London: Macmillan).
HICKS, J. R. (1974) *The Crisis in Keynesian Economics* (Oxford: Blackwell).
HINES, A. G. (1964) 'Trade unions and wage inflation in the United Kingdom 1893–1961', *Review of Economic Studies*, vol. 31, pp. 221–52.
HINES, A. G. (1971) 'The determinants of the rate of change of money wage rates and the effectiveness of incomes policy' in Johnson and Nobay (1971).
HOLDEN, K. and PEEL, D. A. (1985) 'Some empirical evidence on the determinants of incomes policies in the UK', *Economics Letters*, vol. 19, pp. 23–6.
HOLDEN, K., PEEL, D. A. and THOMPSON, J. L. (1985) *Expectations: Theory and Evidence* (London: Macmillan).
HUGHES, W. R. and SILVERSTONE, B. D. J. (1980) 'An assessment of incomes policy in New Zealand: a time series analysis', *Applied Economics*, vol. 12, pp. 467–78.
ILO (1972) *Employment, Incomes and Equality: A Strategy for Increasing Productive Employment in Kenya* (Geneva: International Labour Office).
INGHAM, M. (1981) 'Incomes policy: a short history' in Fallick and Elliott (1981).
ISAAC, J. E. (1972) 'Australian compulsory arbitration and incomes policy' in F. Blackaby (ed.) *An Incomes Policy for Britain* (London: Heinemann).
JACKMAN, R. and KLAPPHOLZ, K. (1975) 'The case for indexing wages and salaries' in Liesner and King (1975).
JACKMAN, R. and LAYARD, R. (1982) 'Trade unions, the NAIRU and a wage-inflation tax', *Economica*, vol. 49, pp. 232–9.
JOHNSON, H. G. and NOBAY, A. R. (eds) (1971) *The Current Inflation* (London: Macmillan).
KARNI, E. (1983) 'On optimal wage indexation', *Journal of Political Economy*, vol. 91, pp. 282–92.

KRAUSE, L. B. and SALANT, W. S. (eds) (1977) *Worldwide Inflation: Theory and Recent Experience* (Washington, D.C.: The Brookings Institution).

LANCASTER, K. (1971) *Consumer Demand: A New Approach* (New York: Columbia University Press).

LANSBURY, R. D. (1978) 'The return to arbitration: recent trends in dispute settlement and wages policy in Australia', *International Labour Review*, vol. 117, no. 5, pp. 611–24.

LAYARD, R. (1982) 'Is incomes policy the answer to unemployment?', *Economica*, vol. 49, pp. 219–32.

LEDINGHAM, P. J. (1973) *An Investigation of the Determinants of Wage and Price Formation in New Zealand* (Wellington: Reserve Bank of New Zealand).

LERNER, A. P. (1978) 'A wage-increase permit plan' in Okun and Perry (1978).

LERNER, A. P. and COLANDER, D. (1980) *MAP – A Market Anti-Inflation Plan* (New York: Harcourt Brace Jovanovich).

LEWIS, W. A. (1954) 'Development with unlimited supplies of labour', *The Manchester School*, vol. 22, pp. 139–91.

LIESNER, T. and KING, M. A. (eds) (1975) *Indexing for Inflation* (London: Heinemann Educational Books).

LIPSEY, R. G. (1960) 'The relation between unemployment and the rate of change of money wage rates in the U.K. 1862–1957: a further analysis', *Economica*, vol. 27, pp. 1–31.

LIPSEY, R. G. and PARKIN, M. (1970) 'Incomes policy: a reappraisal', *Economica*, vol. 37, pp. 1–31.

LOVETT, W. A. (1982) *Inflation and Politics: Fiscal Monetary and Wage-Price Discipline* (Lexington: Lexington Books).

LURIE, S. (1947) *Private Investment in a Controlled Economy* (New York: Columbia University Press).

McCALLUM, B. T. (1975) 'Rational expectations and the natural rate hypothesis: some evidence for the United Kingdom', *The Manchester School*, vol. 43, pp. 56–67.

McCALLUM, B. T. (1976) 'Rational expectations and the natural rate hypothesis', *Econometrica*, vol. 44, pp. 43–52.

McDONALD, I. M. and SOLOW, R. M. (1981) 'Wage bargaining and employment', *American Economic Review*, vol. 71, pp. 896–908.

McFADDEN, D. (1974) 'Conditional logit analysis of qualitative choice behaviour' in P. Zarembka (ed.) *Frontiers in Econometrics* (New York: Academic Press).

MAITAL, S. and BENJAMINI, Y. (1980) 'Inflation as prisoners dilemma', *Journal of Post Keynesian Economics*, vol. 2, pp. 459–81.

MARDLE, R. J. (1968) 'Present methods of wage determination in New Zealand', *New Zealand Economic Papers*, vol. 2, no. 1, pp. 11–37.

MATTHEWS, R. C. O. (1982) 'Comment on the article by Jackman and Layard', *Fiscal Studies*, vol. 3, pp. 61–4.

MAYHEW, K. (1981) 'Incomes policy and the private sector' in Fallick and Elliott (1981).

MEADE, J. E. (1982) *Stagflation Volume 1 Wage Fixing* (London: George Allen and Unwin).

MEADE, J. E. (1985) *Wage Fixing Revisited*, Occasional Paper 72 (London: Institute of Economic Affairs).

MEYER, J. A. (1980) 'Wage and benefit trends under the Carter administration guidelines' in W. Fellner (ed.) *Contemporary Economic Problems 1980* (Washington, D.C.: American Enterprise Institute).

MILLS, D. Q. (1975) *Government, Labor and Inflation: Wage Stabilization in the United States* (Chicago: University of Chicago Press).

MINFORD, A. P. L. (1980) 'A rational expectations model of the UK under fixed and floating exchange rates' in K. Brunner and A. H. Meltzer (eds) *On the State of Macroeconomics*, Carnegie-Rochester Conference Series on Public Policy, vol. 12 (Amsterdam: North-Holland).

MINFORD, A. P. L. and BRECH, M. (1981) 'The wage equation and rational expectations' in D. Currie, R. Nobay and D. Peel (eds) *Macroeconomic Analysis* (London: Croom Helm).

MINFORD, A. P. L. and PEEL, D. A. (1982) 'Tax-based incomes policies: a critique', *Quarterly Economic Bulletin*, Liverpool Research Group in Macroeconomics, February.

MINFORD, A. P. L. and PEEL, D. A. (1983) *Rational Expectations and the New Macroeconomics* (Oxford: Martin Robertson).

MITCHELL, D. J. B. (1984) 'The Australian labour market' in Caves and Krause (1984).

MULVEY, C. (1984) 'Wage policy and wage determination in 1983', *Journal of Industrial Relations*, vol. 26, no. 1, pp. 112–19.

MUSGRAVE, R. A. and MUSGRAVE, P. B. (1980) *Public Finance in Theory and Practice* (New York: McGraw-Hill).

New Zealand Official Yearbook (1984) (Wellington: The Government Printer).

NORDHAUS, W. D. (1981) 'Tax-based incomes policies: a better mousetrap' in M. P. Claudon and R. R. Cornwall (eds) *An Incomes Policy for the United States* (Boston: Martinus Nijhoff).

NORMAN, N. R. (1976) *The Prices Justification Tribunal: Stage Two* (Canberra: Australian Industries Development Association).

NUTI, D. M. (1969) 'On incomes policy', *Science and Society*, vol. 33, pp. 415–25.

OI, W. Y. (1976) 'On measuring the impact of wage–price controls: a critical appraisal' in Brunner and Meltzer (1976).

OKUN, A. M. (1977) 'The great stagflation swamp', *Challenge*, vol. 20, November/December, p. 13.

OKUN, A. M. and PERRY, G. L. (eds) (1978) *Curing Chronic Inflation* (Washington: The Brookings Institution).

PAGE, S. (1975) 'International experience of indexing' in Liesner and King (1975).

PALEKAR, S. A. (1962) *Problems of Wage Policy for Economic Development* (London: Asia Publishing House).

PARKIN, J. M. (1979) 'Alternative explanations of UK inflation: a survey' in J. M. Parkin and M. Sumner (eds) *Inflation in the UK* (Manchester: Manchester University Press).

PARKIN, J. M. and SUMNER, M. (eds) (1972) *Incomes Policy and Inflation* (Manchester: Manchester University Press).

PARKIN, J. M., SUMNER, M. and JONES, R. A. (1972) 'A survey of the econometric evidence of the effects of incomes policy on the rate of inflation' in Parkin and Sumner (1972).

PARKIN, M., SUMNER, M. and WARD, R. (1976) 'The effects of excess demand, generalised expectations and wage–price controls on wage inflation in the U.K. 1956–71' in Brunner and Meltzer (1976).

PAZNER, E. A. (1981) 'On indexation and macroeconomic stability' in M. J. Flanders and A. Razin (eds) *Development in an Inflationary World* (New York: Academic Press).

PEEL, D. A. (1979) 'The dynamic behaviour of a simple macroeconomic model with a tax-based incomes policy', *Economics Letters*, vol. 3, pp. 139–43.

PENCAVEL, J. H. (1981) 'The American experience with incomes policies' in Fallick and Elliott (1981).

PERRY, G. L. (1967) 'Wage and price guideposts', *American Economic Review*, vol. 57, pp. 897–904.

PERRY, G. L. (1970) 'Changing labor markets and inflation', *Brookings Papers on Economic Activity*, pp. 411–48.

PHELPS, E. S. (1970) 'Money wage dynamics and labour market equilibrium' in E. S. Phelps (ed.) *Microeconomic Foundations of Employment and Inflation Theory* (London: Macmillan).

PINDYCK, R. S. and RUBINFELD, D. (1981) *Econometric Models and Economic Forecasts* (New York: McGraw-Hill).

PLOWMAN, D. H. (1981) *Wage Indexation* (London: George Allen and Unwin).

REID, F. (1979) 'The effects of controls on the rate of wage change in Canada', *Canadian Journal of Economics*, vol. 12, pp. 214–27.

REID, F. (1981) 'Control and decontrol of wages in the United States', *American Economic Review*, vol. 71, pp. 108–20.

ROBINSON, D. and MAYHEW, K. (1983) *Pay Policies for the Future* (Oxford: Oxford University Press).

ROSE, W. D. (1972) 'The regulation of wages and prices as part of macroeconomic policy', *Quarterly Predictions of National Income and Expenditure (NZIER)*, no. 30, pp. 14–18.

SARGAN, J. D. (1964) 'Wages and prices in the United Kingdom' in P. E. Hart, G. Mills and J. K. Whitaker (eds) *Econometric Analysis for National Economic Planning* (London: Butterworths).

SARGENT, T. J. (1979) *Macroeconomic Theory* (New York: Academic Press).

SCARTH, W. M. (1983) 'Tax-related incomes policies and macroeconomic stability', *Journal of Macroeconomics*, vol. 5, no. 1, pp. 91–103.

SCHOENBAUM, D. (1967) *Hitlers Social Revolution* (London: Weidenfeld and Nicolson).

SCHUETTINGER, R. (1982) 'A survey of wage and price controls over fifty centuries' in M. Walker (ed.) *Tax-Based Incomes Policies: A Cure for Inflation?* (Vancouver: Fraser Institute).

SCHWEITZER, A. (1964) *Big Business in the Third Reich* (London: Eyre and Spottiswoode).

SEIDMAN, L. S. (1976) 'A payroll tax-credit to restrain inflation', *National Tax Journal*, vol. 29, pp. 398–412.

SEIDMAN, L. S. (1978) 'Tax-based incomes policies', *Brookings Papers on Economic Activity*, pp. 301–48, also in Okun and Perry (1978).

SHAVELL, S. (1976) 'Sharing risks of deferred payment', *Journal of Political Economy*, vol. 84, pp. 161–8.

SIMLER, N. J. and TELLA, A. (1968) 'Labour reserves and the Phillips curve', *Review of Economics and Statistics*, vol. 50, pp. 32–49.

SLITOR, R. E. (1979) 'Implementation and design of tax-based incomes policies', *American Economic Review*, Papers and Proceedings, vol. 69, no. 2, May, pp. 212–5.

SMITH, A. D. (ed.) (1969) *Wage Policy Issues in Economic Development* (London: Macmillan).

SMITH, D. C. (1972) 'Incomes policy' in Parkin and Sumner (1972) abridged from R. E. Caves (ed.) *Britain's Economic Prospects* (Washington, D.C.: The Brookings Institution).

STEVENS, C. M. (1966) 'Is compulsory arbitration compatible with bargaining?', *Industrial Relations*, vol. 5, pp. 38–52.

SUMNER, M. and WARD, R. (1983) 'The reappearing Phillips curve', *Oxford Economic Papers* (Supplement), vol. 35, pp. 306–20.

TARLING, R. and WILKINSON, F. (1977) 'The Social Contract: postwar incomes policies and their inflationary impact', *Cambridge Journal of Economics*, vol. 1, pp. 395–414.

TAYLOR, J. (1970) 'Hidden unemployment, hoarded labour and the Phillips curve', *Southern Economic Journal*, vol. 37, pp. 1–16.

TAYLOR, J. B. (1980) 'Aggregate dynamics and staggered contracts', *Journal of Political Economy*, vol. 88, pp. 1–23.

TOBIN, J. and HOUTHAKKER, H. (1951) 'The effects of rationing on consumer demands', *Review of Economic Studies*, vol. 18, pp. 140–53.

TURNOVSKY, S. J. (1977) *Macroeconomic Analysis and Stabilization Policies* (Cambridge: Cambridge University Press).

TURNOVSKY, S. J. (1983) 'Wage indexation and exchange market intervention in a small open economy', *Canadian Journal of Economics*, vol. 16, pp. 574–92.

ULMAN, L. and FLANAGAN, R. J. (1971) *Wage Restraint: A Study of Incomes Policies in Western Europe* (Berkeley: University of California Press).

WALLICH, H. C. and WEINTRAUB, S. (1971) 'A tax-based incomes policy', *Journal of Economic Issues*, vol. 5, no. 2, pp. 1–19.

WALLIS, K. F. (1971) 'Wages, prices and incomes policies: some comments', *Economica*, vol. 38, pp. 304–10.

WEITZMAN, M. L. (1983) 'Some macroeconomic implications of alternative compensation systems', *Economic Journal*, vol. 93, pp. 763–83.

WEITZMAN, M. L. (1984) *The Share Economy: Conquering Inflation* (Cambridge, Mass.: Harvard University Press).

WOOD, J. (1985) 'Last offer arbitration', *British Journal of Industrial Relations*, vol. 23, pp. 415–24.

Author Index

Subject Index

143